THE BOOK
of LIFE

First published in 2022 by
The Dedalus Press
13 Moyclare Road
Baldoyle
Dublin D13 K1C2
Ireland

www.dedaluspress.com

ISBN 978-1-915629-07-4 (paperback)
ISBN 978-1-915629-06-7 (hardback)

Dedalus Press titles are available in Ireland
from Argosy Books (www.argosybooks.ie) and in the UK
from Inpress Books (www.inpressbooks.co.uk)

Cover image: *L.nuge* / Shutterstock

The Dedalus Press receives financial assistance from
The Arts Council / An Chomhairle Ealaíon.

THE BOOK
of LIFE

Poems To Tide You Over

Edited by
GRACE WELLS

DEDALUS PRESS

Contents

⌒

PART ONE

Poem for a Birth: Grace Wells ⌒ 13
What I Remember: Ann Joyce ⌒ 13
Umbilicus: Mary Montague ⌒ 14
Clair de Lune: Jessica Traynor ⌒ 16
The Gift: Paula Meehan ⌒ 16
This December: Paul Perry ⌒ 17
On Tickling: Mary O'Donoghue ⌒ 19
July: Ross Thompson ⌒ 19
Home: Enda Wyley ⌒ 20
The Boy with the Kite: Paul Perry ⌒ 20
Struck: Ross Thompson ⌒ 22
Running Away from Home: Gerry Murphy ⌒ 23
Alphabet Soup: Michael Augustin ⌒ 24
Alliteration: Iggy McGovern ⌒ 24
Ocean Letters: Joseph Woods ⌒ 25
Watching Cable News: John Kelly ⌒ 26
The Bad Boys' House: Ross Thompson ⌒ 26
The Rub: Paula Meehan ⌒ 27
The Hostage Place: Grace Wells ⌒ 28
Friends: Patrick Deeley ⌒ 29
Twelve: Catherine Ann Cullen ⌒ 29
The Clock Tower: John O'Donnell ⌒ 30
And Everything was Possible: Ruy Belo ⌒ 31

PART TWO

from 'Orpheus': Theo Dorgan ⌒ 32
Somewhere on Barnes Common a Box of Chocolates:
    Grace Wells ⌒ 33

Playmates: John O'Donnell ⌒ 34
Aimsir Chaite / Past Tense: Doireann Ní Ghríofa ⌒ 35
My Aunt Reads the Tarot: Jessica Traynor ⌒ 36
The Bonnet: Paula Meehan ⌒ 37
Lining Out: Pat Boran ⌒ 38
Witches: Enda Coyle-Greene ⌒ 39
Rave / Rave: Doireann Ní Ghríofa ⌒ 41
Confidante: Erin Fornoff ⌒ 42
I'm On Fire: Ross Thompson ⌒ 43
Tent: Pat Boran ⌒ 44
The Gaeltacht: John Kelly ⌒ 45
Tree House: Erin Fornoff ⌒ 45

PART THREE

In Your Own Dreamtime: Lynn Caldwell ⌒ 47
Argentina: Patrick Kehoe ⌒ 48
Panda: Jennifer Matthews ⌒ 48
Rue St Paul: Mary Noonan ⌒ 49
Remnants: Ross Thompson ⌒ 51
Passover: Ben Keatinge ⌒ 52
Hearing *The Boatman's Call* in a Boston Laundromat:
    Doireann Ní Ghríofa ⌒ 52
Wintering: Paul Perry ⌒ 54
Footfall: Celeste Augé ⌒ 55
While Bleeding: Doireann Ní Ghríofa ⌒ 57
What Woke Up: Polina Cosgrave ⌒ 58
Excursion: Ann Zell ⌒ 58
The Road Out: Lynn Caldwell ⌒ 60
Rooted: Victoria Melkovska ⌒ 60
32 Kg Suitcase: Rafael Mendes ⌒ 61

PART FOUR

Choice: Gerry Murphy ✎ 63
Valentine: Mary Noonan ✎ 63
I Will Gabble: Mary Noonan ✎ 64
'A Boatman Loses His Oars': Sone No Yoshitada ✎ 65
In Ikea: Doireann Ní Ghríofa ✎ 66
The Map: Yau Noi ✎ 66
Swans: Katherine Duffy ✎ 67
Tomorrow: Tom Mathews ✎ 68
Laburnum: Paula Meehan ✎ 69
Storm: Agnieszka Filipek ✎ 71
I Am the Woman: Ulla Hahn ✎ 71
Random Cataloguing: Gerry Murphy ✎ 72
'Other Than You': Gyoson ✎ 73
The Ring: Paul Perry ✎ 73
Hair Piece: Mark Roper ✎ 74
The Plan: Pat Boran ✎ 75
Honeymoon: Gerard Smyth ✎ 75
Love Song: Eleanor Hooker ✎ 76

PART FIVE

Guest in Reverse: Joseph Woods ✎ 77
Free Dive: Polina Cosgrave ✎ 78
Míreanna Mearaí / Jigsaw: Doireann Ní Ghríofa ✎ 79
Threading the Light: Ross Thompson ✎ 80
You Were Born in an Ark: Christian Wethered ✎ 81
Atlas: Mary Mullen ✎ 82
Sólás / Solace: Doireann Ní Ghríofa ✎ 83
Taisí / Remains: Ceaití Ní Bheildiúin ✎ 84
Child Burial: Paula Meehan ✎ 87
Firelight: Mark Roper ✎ 89

PART SIX

Scooter: Catherine Ann Cullen ⌇ 91
Let's Die: Pat Boran ⌇ 92
Night Before School: Catherine Ann Cullen ⌇ 94
Leictreachas Statach / Static Electrictiy:
    Doireann Ní Ghríofa ⌇ 95
Cocoon: Doireann Ní Ghríofa ⌇ 96
The Lone Parent Does Not Write: Grace Wells ⌇ 97
My Mother's Getaway: Patrick Deeley ⌇ 98
A Woman of Anglo-Ireland: Mark Roper ⌇ 99
Ex-Voto: Grace Wells ⌇ 100
The Children of Alcoholics: Pat Boran ⌇ 101
A Mother Mourns Her Heroin-Addicted Daughter:
    Leland Bardwell ⌇ 102
Aegis: Grace Wells ⌇ 103
The Nest: Richard Tillinghast ⌇ 104
A Sapling Birch: Francis Harvey ⌇ 105

PART SEVEN

And suddenly you're at that place: Enda Coyle-Greene ⌇ 106
After Ophelia: Emma Must ⌇ 107
Tomorrow: Mikiro Sasaki ⌇ 107
Going to the Well: Mutsuo Takahashi ⌇ 109
A Meeting in Naju's Bar: Hanyong Jeong ⌇ 110
Weekend Away: John Kelly ⌇ 111
After the Holiday: Mark Roper ⌇ 112
Intruder: Pat Boran ⌇ 113
In Our Stairwell: Gennady Alexeyev ⌇ 115
Night Start: Paddy Bushe ⌇ 116
Gravity: Mark Roper ⌇ 117
Postcard from Hospital: Paddy Bushe ⌇ 118
Red Mouse: Enda Wyley ⌇ 118
Visiting the Locked Ward: Tom Mathews ⌇ 119

'Such A Life They Think': Kisen ⮑ 120
Estuary: Pat Boran ⮑ 120
The Broken Fields: Mark Roper ⮑ 121
Seas Siar / Stand Back: Ceaití Ní Bheildiúin ⮑ 121
Blessings: Francis Harvey ⮑ 123
The Red Dogs of Wicklow: Paul Perry ⮑ 124
Closure: Grace Wells ⮑ 125
The Things We Keep: Gerard Smyth ⮑ 126
Skip: Mark Roper ⮑ 127
The Moons: Paula Meehan ⮑ 128
In Ireland, I: Mutsuo Takahashi ⮑ 128
In Praise of Pottering: Mark Roper ⮑ 129

PART EIGHT

Your Native Home: Giuliano Nistri ⮑ 130
The Daily Crossword: Ross Thompson ⮑ 131
The Meadow: Ann Joyce ⮑ 132
My Father Perceived as a Vision of St. Francis:
    Paula Meehan ⮑ 133
Wilson: John O'Donnell ⮑ 134
Holiday Home: Joseph Woods ⮑ 135
Body: Mary Noonan ⮑ 136
Red Shoe: Katherine Duffy ⮑ 137
Bedside Locker: Joseph Woods ⮑ 138
Sea Fret: Mark Roper ⮑ 139
Cherries: Catherine Ann Cullen ⮑ 140
Hands: Chris Jones ⮑ 141
The Hands: Paula Meehan ⮑ 142
Putting the Clocks Forward: John Kelly ⮑ 142
The Old Professor: Paula Meehan ⮑ 143
Swing: Paddy Bushe ⮑ 144
Salt Over the Shoulder: Annie Deppe ⮑ 145
Watching How It Happens: Francis Harvey ⮑ 145

'What Use Your Bright': Ono No Komachi ⌒ 146

Saturday Morning: Mark Roper ⌒ 146

Love in the Glen: Francis Harvey ⌒ 148

Seasons: Patrick Deeley ⌒ 148

Afternoon in Olhao: Paddy Bushe ⌒ 149

05:40: Paddy Bushe ⌒ 149

Neighbours: Sally Wheeler ⌒ 150

All This: Knut Ødegård ⌒ 150

In May The Park And Me Revisited: Macdara Woods ⌒ 152

PART NINE

Winter Funeral: Pádraig J. Daly ⌒ 154

Plans: Eva Bourke ⌒ 154

Public: Mark Roper ⌒ 157

Cold: Mark Roper ⌒ 158

Mother Died Yesterday: Eriko Tsugawa-Madden ⌒ 158

Ever: Richard Tillinghast ⌒ 159

Lost and Found: Pat Boran ⌒ 160

Sin-Eater: Jessica Traynor ⌒ 161

The Shoe Box Coffin: Catherine Ann Cullen ⌒ 162

The Inscription: Paula Meehan ⌒ 163

A Single Rose: Leland Bardwell ⌒ 163

Anniversary: Mark Roper ⌒ 164

Winter Coat: Leeanne Quinn ⌒ 165

Marbhna Oisín / Lament for Oisín: Paddy Bushe ⌒ 165

In Memory of Naoise 1993–2002: Francis Harvey ⌒ 166

'No Road Beyond The Graveyard': Leland Bardwell ⌒ 167

On the Hill, My Tomb, Marine Cemetery: Landa Wo ⌒ 168

The Olive Tree: Mutsuo Takahashi ⌒ 169

⌒

ACKNOWLEDGEMENTS & THANKS ⌒ 170

INTRODUCTION

The best poetry is a form of spiritual autobiography – poems that stand as way-markers along a poet's soul journey. Such poems tend to narrate a particular life-experience, but somehow in their telling, they touch the soul of the reader. They remind us not so much of a shared experience but rather a shared knowing. They resonate with a mood or tone within ourselves that we instantly recognise as true. Such potent writing is a rare thing, but the poems gathered here are such poems – way-markers and turning points along the journey of our becoming. Each one captures an important rite of passage, or the closure or beginning of a personal epoch. Though the experience may be unique to its author, the poems resonate with a far wider sense of soul knowledge.

These tender and, I think, invaluable poems have all been drawn from the extensive range of Dedalus Press titles in print. Principally the work has been harvested from a wide range of contemporary poets writing in Ireland today both in English and Irish. But there are also poems in translation from across Europe and the Far East. Perhaps most movingly there are poems from beloved poets no longer with us, the recently deceased, and those lost to us centuries ago but whose work still speaks to the enduring nature of the human condition. The collected poems span eons and traverse geographies to converse about the nature of life. They lay bare the great transitions we must each pass through, and honour the smallest rites of passage that deeply impact the soul along its journey. At times the poets differ with and contradict each other, but their many voices build to reveal essential truths we can each resonate with.

I cannot claim that all life is here, but much of it is. There are poems of wonder and challenge, joy and tragedy. As the poets pass through their different life phases, there is often the poignant and unwelcome surrender of an earlier self, a giving-up of something lovely and innocent and free. The poems speak of pain and loneliness. But word by word, the rhythms and intimacies of these poems lull us down beneath our suffering, to our stillness and receptivity. They shine light into our becoming, and reveal the wisdom, maturity and compassion that life ultimately engenders. Loneliness gives way to a deeper sense of companionship and shared endeavour.

Each time I read this anthology I feel myself in the company of a good friend. I hope that becomes true for other readers, that this little book of large-hearted poems becomes in time a treasured object, a dog-eared, much-loved companion for life. It is not the voice of one particular poet that we come away with, but rather the collective voice of our shared humanity. In our era of division that daily invites us to mistrust one another, to condemn strangers and shun or cancel those who think differently from ourselves, it seems particularly vital to me that we reassert and rekindle our mutuality. That we act from our commonality. For me that is the abiding note this collection sets onto the air – the harmony of human goodness resonates through these poems from every page.

— Grace Wells

PART ONE

POEM FOR A BIRTH

In her arms the stars appear,
and deep in her winter earth
the seedlings stir and waken green.
Everything broken can be remade,
and her child is ever a source of wonder.

GRACE WELLS (b. 1968)

WHAT I REMEMBER

Who can remember the first year
let alone the first hour? All I can do
is imagine myself swimming in a bubble

round and round inside my mother,
my body curled like a fist, my mother
doing time, counting months, then days.

A summer baby, the wild pain,
room bristling with birth-cries.
You get used to it, this gift of child.

I imagine I drooled over her summer
dress, the small daisy print my earth,
holding tight to myself that small part

of self I could never let go, not even
to her warm arms nestling me,
holding me as she would a china cup.

What I do remember is my mother
standing at the table by the window,
the oil lamp hanging above her

like her off-centre halo,
my hands holding the sides
of a cradle my father had fashioned,

singing about going to *Amer-ge-go*,
ready even then to fly the coop.

ANN JOYCE (b. 1946)

UMBILICUS

Days
when it felt
like it would throttle me
like a noose.

Days
when I fought its lasso
as desperately
as a feral horse.

Once free
I thought I would run forever
my feet bruised and throbbing
from the roughness
of the ground between us.

Days
I thought you were lost
to me as I was
to you.

Now
little can repair
the damage done.

Our house
will not be restored
but still
we live in it.

Between us
stretches that silver cord
shining as when it held us
bound
in the amniotic lair.

MARY MONTAGUE (b. 1964)

CLAIR DE LUNE

I see the moon
and the moon sees me –
my mother's face
over mine,
some long-forgotten evening.

But what has been lost
in the space of those years?

That cool, uncluttered moonlight,
the syllables of song
that settled on us both;
and the clarity of seeing,
being seen.

JESSICA TRAYNOR (b. 1984)

THE GIFT

My godmother on her deathbed gave
up this memory of me aged two
in my grandmother Mary's garden
about the time I first got language.
Like a queen who rules all she surveys
I'm saying *nice nice nice* as I wave
to bee, fly, worm, wasp, bird, to the blue
cloudless sky, at home in creation,
my realm bordered by sweet privet hedge.

PAULA MEEHAN (b. 1955)

THIS DECEMBER

my bed
a magic carpet
and
the curtains left
a little askew
onto Three Rock
and
its darkness
opened
I lay down
into the weave
and
exhaled
and watched
my breath
draw colour
from the hills
and watched
my father
and mother
grow small
from the toil
it had taken
to build
such a carpet
as this.

PAUL PERRY (b. 1972)

17

ON TICKLING

We cannot tickle ourselves.
Failed mission, a niggle

and prod between bars
of the rib-cage, ouching

ourselves with the same
indignation of smarting

skin when a scab
is pulled too soon

from its smooch
of a wound.

So we need the hands
of others, guitarists

to start a jazzy strum,
to riff the rungs

on that ladder of bone,
tinkle our ivories

with oh-so-acute
attention to the note

struck from floating
spars, broken bars

at the bottom, until
we curl foetal,

spineless hedgehog,
a ball of squealing,

hating, and wanting
another arpeggio.

MARY O'DONOGHUE (b. 1975)

JULY

By a horseshoe bay – calm, clean and ringed by green fields –
we squeeze the last drops from a postcard holiday

spent by the sea. Through glassy memory and dream,
time curves like liquid. You ebb towards me then flow

away. I tightrope walk the sharp teeth of the beach,
combing for treasure, weighing shells, measuring stones

and digging to Australia with my toy spade.
I can see you wringing your fingers and smoothing

down a pencil skirt whipped by the breeze. I can hear
you calling my name, warning me about cutting

my bare toes on crab claws ... straying ... breaking the
    chain ...
then the film fades to black and the loop starts again.

ROSS THOMPSON (b. 1975)

HOME

If I could go back, it would be to there –
early summer and I would be barefoot,
the line of hot tar in the middle of the road
bubbling under my toes, the tree's blossoms
a spread of pink below our bedroom window.

There's the squawk of gulls rising up
from the fish at Dún Laoghaire pier,
the squeal of children leaping over
the hedge nets of back garden play –
The more you eat, the more you jump…

There's the sun through the kitchen window,
glinting on my mother's hair;
she swivels from a full sink,
scattering suds and laughter
as she bends to me.

If I could go back, it would be to there –
those rooms, the smell of dinner.
Key in the lock, our father calls, *Home…*
Night bringing its skillet of dreams,
our ticking clock wound tight.

ENDA WYLEY (b. 1966)

THE BOY WITH THE KITE

three cars are parked on the beach
a dog is running to and from the shore

20

chasing the tide out and scampering
away as it returns lovers walk with lazy steps

a girl with ponytails dances with two
handfuls of sand but the boy with the kite

sees none of it not even the sea
blue and green and black moving

his gaze is turned skyward where a kite
a flame moves like an ancient dancer

a soul on a string waving and flinching
and diving like a frantic seagull into the unknown

all day people have fished and surfed
walked and believed in all manner

of miracle cars ice cream the resurrection
of the body but for the boy with the kite

there is only one prayer he doesn't hear
the dog bark he doesn't see the dropping sun

or hear the sound of night like an alarm
bell ringing over and over he's a lone dancer

a devotee to the beauty of flight
an admirer to the ballet of aeronautics

he can keep it there the kite still
like a humming bird so you can't even see

its wings fluttering at speed he they the boy
with the kite the boy and the kite

are a poem in the making and when he
walks away in the sky above him

in its eternal blueness the kite pivots and burns

PAUL PERRY

STRUCK

My grandfather was a big man who filled
a room with fables that caught the true wind
like a coloured mainsail and set our course
for South America: me on his knee,

manning the wheel; him at stern, bellowing
encouraging words as we braved a storm
that rose up from below. The kraken's tail
whipped our ship. Lightning forked the mast. A thread

of ice drew a dividing line between
two annexed sides of his body. A whole
bank of circuit breakers broke, went to sleep
and never awoke. Slumped in his armchair,

he shrunk smaller than a vanishing star.
His mouth, now an adit to a collapsed mine,
whispered bits of words that failed to tell
how far his mind was torn by civil war.

Thereafter, our ship remained locked in port.

ROSS THOMPSON

RUNNING AWAY FROM HOME

I have been playing all afternoon
with my brother and sister,
during which I have managed
to upset one of our neighbours
by running through his rose garden.
He threatens to inform my mother;
no need, my brother and sister
are already running to tell her.
When I get to the front gate,
I can see they have told her everything.
'Wait till I get you inside,'
she calls from the front door;
from the top of the steps
I make my announcement:
'I'm running away from home
and I'm never coming back!'
'Off you go,' she replies.
'Don't forget to write,'
she calls after me
as I take to my heels.
About fifty yards from the house,
on the hill leading down
to the main road,
the presbytery looms
in the gathering darkness,
its stand of cypress trees
soughing and creaking
in a freshening breeze.
Daunted, I turn tail
and run back home.
When I knock at the front door
my mother answers.

'You didn't get far and you never wrote,'
she says, my promised beating
forgotten in her helpless laughter.

GERRY MURPHY (b. 1952)

ALPHABET SOUP

Before I started school, I used to love alphabet soup.
Precisely and only because the initial letters of my first
and last names were swimming in there. The rest of the
alphabet consisted of meaningless noodles.

MICHAEL AUGUSTIN (b. 1953)
Translated from the German by Sujata Bhatt

ALLITERATION

When the boy from the Soldiers' Cottages
allowed that I was a "Fuckin' Fenian"
and clipped my ear, I ran home faster
than speeding bullets, where, narrow-eyed,
my mother clipped the other ear
for using such "lavatory language".
And that was also the very same year
I trod on an up-turned six-inch nail
that pierced my sole, and my mother's heart,
as she set to work with Dettol and plaster,
all the while murmuring "Christ crucified"!

And something else that formed a veil
like a gas cloud rolling over the rampart:
The murderous "Gang Green".

IGGY MCGOVERN (b. 1948)

OCEAN LETTERS

I must have been eight when I got my first room
across from the kitchen downstairs, narrow
and windowless, but I loved it for its being
at the heart of things. Our backdoor
faced front, so in bed I could hear

everything – conversations, whispered send-offs
from older siblings, a neighbour's souped-up
car changing gear and sounding off into the night –
or simply follow stars through the skylight,
imagining myself in some ship's open hold

while Morse code drifted in from the kitchen,
my brother tapping the keys of an oscillator
into the dots and dashes of messages,
Secret and *Plain Language*, *Mayday Relays*
and *Ocean Letters*, preparing for the exam
that would never quite set him to sea.

JOSEPH WOODS (b. 1966)

WATCHING CABLE NEWS

We built our forts with hazel rods
and canopies of fern,
and sometimes a fire would be lit –
as fires have always been lit –
in a ring of blackened stones.
We'd sit together on the beaten clay.
Some smoked Woodbine. Some longed for rain.

Next day, you'd come upon the wreckage.
Enemy attack? Elephants on the rampage?
No. Just boys. Sometimes the same boys
who had built the thing, the same boys
who crushed the eggs of waterhens
and tortured fish.

Even at the age of ten I would despair –
I'd curse humanity to Hell
and thrash the homeward hedges
with a broken switch.

JOHN KELLY (b. 1965)

THE BAD BOYS' HOUSE

On Sunday afternoons you took long walks
with your parents by the open air pool,
outdoor gospel pews, smuggler's cove, fun park
and those leafy avenues where you stole
conkers. You felt you were an imposter
in this closed off realm of old world grandeur.
One street was marked by a dark house: a swear

word scrawled on a kerb that caught your young eye
and made you flush. Your mum said it was where
bad boys were sent when disobedient.
You, clean-living and innocent as snow,
thought of those bad boys at school who lied, stole
and doled out beatings without a second
thought: dead arms, "Red Hands of Ulster", lashes
with the wetted ends of tightly-bound towels.
A litany of welts and bruises
that cut right to your bones: a reminder
of who owned you; how your home was never
too far away from the reach of bad boys
inured to using knives and words and stones.
And that fear: what if you were ever caught
doing something you should not? Or accused
with a charge that was patently untrue?
You would not last a day in that borstal.
They would chew you into tiny morsels.

ROSS THOMPSON

THE RUB

It was what she'd say when things got rough
back there in Thebes Central – the kitchen –
where it never came out in the wash,
the one original stain, the sin
of the fathers spun down through the years.
Every word she hurled could pierce the skin:
she could talk common, she could talk posh.
I sat like a stone growing lichen.
What didn't kill me would make me tough.

PAULA MEEHAN

THE HOSTAGE PLACE

Invisible the insect held within the amber of our father's boat.
Hull he built himself, condensing his finest fibres into
     boards
that bore the lick of sun and wave until their taught wood sang.

Evening light could strike its umber sail to flame, light a vision
that denied the bite of rope, of salt, the angry sting, for, though
the rudder steered, our father drove with a lashing tongue. And

I never wanted to feel the look upon my mother's face
     upon my own.
That horizon gaze which stared beyond and saw nothing
left each of us unable to find a course out from his dark hold.

Each of us still able to inhabit the place we'd crawl: that
     prow locker,
cupboard for pump and bailer, anchor, and metal chain
     that clinked
into each wave, where to the kind sound of water receiving
     wood

we learned to sleep,
cheeks pressed into the life vest's sweating, yellow flesh.

GRACE WELLS

FRIENDS

Me and PJ. PJ and me. Whichever way I put it
sounded good. Ran, raided, hurled, fought –
all one. Slugged the altar wine behind Fr. Doran's back.
Knocked the heads off tulips parading
along by Teacher's wall. Bathed in Keaveney's Well,
which half the village drew on for drinking.
Adventured. Until the May evening in Mullagh Beg
when a tinker lad stood on the sideline,
watching us hurlers train. "Get rid of 'im,"
our reffing mentor barked in my direction. I gaped
at the red-lidded watery eyes, the snotted sleeve,
the sawn-off wellingtons banding black
chafe-marks – *iroch* – across his spindly shanks,
and changed my mind. PJ said I was chicken – "Just
watch this." He waded in with hurley flailing,
battered that tinker lad down. "They're the same
as animals," he shrugged, when someone
chided him about doing the dirt. But I knew it would
never be PJ and me, me and PJ again. Not
that I was any better than him, merely the recognition
of my own soft spot, open to the world's hurt.

PATRICK DEELEY (b. 1953)

TWELVE

Twelve is a foothold in a foreign town;
A ledge you lie on to look down
On childish things, and out at you-know-what;
Bras whether you need them or not;

Knickers and nerves to get in a knot.
Twelve's a bridge from end to edge;
The wafer of the grown-up wedge;
A walk with a hint of hip;
A mouth that gives everyone lip
Glossily; a fossily child in a woman's stone;
A bitter pill with bright pink sugar on it;
A whole poem, two lines shy of a sonnet.

CATHERINE ANN CULLEN (b. 1961)

THE CLOCK TOWER

Rung by rung we climbed, ascending into what seemed
a kind of heaven, the school's clock tower strictly out of
    bounds,
the pleasure in the lung-constricting terror, knowing the fall
would kill us. But we knew little else, and dying was so
    far off,
further than the dizzying football fields, the cars below
    like toys,
the matchbox houses lighting one by one the autumn
    evening,
and beyond all this the sea, clutching her frozen souls.
We were immortal then, untidy ink-stained gods
watching from on high, above time's granite certainties,
the steel hands of the clock-face like all schoolboys
never quite telling the truth, but set instead a little fast,
as if what lay ahead for us would not come soon enough.

JOHN O'DONNELL (b. 1960)

AND EVERYTHING WAS POSSIBLE

When I was still young before I left home
all eager to travel around the world
I already knew about the waves' breaking
from the pages of all the books I'd read

When May rolled around everything was flowers
the morning turtledove flew here flew there
and to hear the dreamer just speak of life
was like having it actually happen

Everything took place in another life
and there was always a way out when needed
When was all of this? Not even I know
I know only that I had a child's power
all things were close to me and everything
was possible I only had to want it

RUY BELO (1933–1978)
Translalted from the Portuguese by Richard Zenith

PART TWO

"I would go back, but the ways are winding,
  If ways there are to that land, in sooth;
  For what man succeeds in ever finding
  A path to the garden of his lost youth?"
—Ella Wheeler Wilcox, 'The Lost Garden'

from 'ORPHEUS'

I stand back from the streetlight at her school gate,
I make myself invisible, blood pulsing
in raised veins. Exams are near, she's studying late.
My first brush with fate –

I am all attention, my nerves electric.
Breathing is difficult, couldn't answer to what
I am doing here; driven or drawn, can't tell which,
fear I might be sick …

These days, likely someone would call the police.
I'd stop myself, would take a careful look at
the staring boy, dense in his concentration,
so clearly obsessed –

and that was me at seventeen, some grey twist
in my head, shot through with fires of rage and hope,
gambling for my salvation on the one cool
glance I feared to miss.

THEO DORGAN (b. 1953)

SOMEWHERE ON BARNES COMMON
A BOX OF CHOCOLATES

The boys who rode into our Eden were rough,
we had the sense not to give them our addresses –
bad enough they'd found our favourite tree

where all summer we'd sprawled like lionesses
uncaring of any world below,
afternoons spent in serious talk of what awaited,

only to jump back onto our bikes, to speed
from the future's grasp, dodging the Common's
scrubby bushes, defying gravity, inviolate.

Their leader took a shine to me, and persisted,
shaking us from branch to earth, so we'd arrive
to find them, languid as panthers, in our place.

Cast out we had no choice but to let them in,
though all was changed, we shared a Common tongue.
He brought me chocolates in a sealed box,

I would have dared their dark shell, bit eager teeth
into the sweet, white flesh, only my sister
said he'd stolen them. She banked on fear, threatened

the police, insisted the evidence be thrown away.
I leant upon the wisdom of her age, half-sensed
a jealous hiss behind her care. No matter that I didn't eat

them then, nor how far my young arm threw that box,
distance couldn't shield me; the contents bore my name,
kisses, betrayals, desire's complications: love in all its forms.

GRACE WELLS

PLAYMATES

Under eaves adorned with Goldwing
and Led Zep, The Owls' First Team,
we gathered in grey flannel to thumb dog-eared
magazines that Suds' elder brother kept stashed
beneath the narrow unmade bed. So much there

for all of us to learn, our schoolbags
slingstones hurled below us as we thundered
up the stairs, a herd of hormones on stampede
to this top room. A window gave out onto the street
as we gave in to Playmates, Readers' Wives,

the curves and limbs of honeyed ladies awaiting
walnut-muscled men; and, once, a gatefold
of two women embracing, naked, mouths shaped
in a perfect O as they moved in for the kiss. "Lezzers,"
proclaimed Donut, whose brother worked at weekends

in the European Film Club. The room swam.
We drowned for hours in dreams of glossy flesh

until we heard the song of Suds' Mum, Orpheus
in an apron, calling through the flames
of oven gas mark five for Suds to come down

for his tea. The door-latch clicked behind us
like an empty gun as we left, crossing towards the bus-stop
to begin the long fall home, girls in spring-green uniforms
cavorting round that maypole while we stood at a safe distance,
rooted, helpless as young trees, the sap rising, rising.

JOHN O'DONNELL

AIMSIR CHAITE

Trasna an tseomra
ar thonnta lámh,
seolann sé nótaí chugam.

Sa choirnéal graifítí
ar chúl na scoile
fanann sé orm,
blas tobac ar a bheola.

Le sciorta craptha suas thar glúine nochta,
caithim mo mhála scoile ar leataobh,
lán le hobair bhaile gan tosú –
leathanaigh fholmha
ar bhriathra neamhrialta
san aimsir fháistineach.

DOIREANN NÍ GHRÍOFA (b. 1981)

PAST TENSE

On a wave of palms,
his words float over the class
to reach my hand.

He pauses behind the school, waiting
by the wall most fluent in graffiti-scrawl.
His fingers drum. His tongue tastes
of smoke and chewing gum.

My skirt is rolled up over bare knees
when I arrive and fling my schoolbag
aside, full of homework I haven't started
yet – page after empty page to be filled
with irregular verbs
of the future tense.

DOIREANN NÍ GHRÍOFA

MY AUNT READS THE TAROT

She frowns at my mother,
fans the cards across our vinyl table cloth.
They make a sound like sighing,
as if they have secrets
too terrible to disclose.

My aunt's face pauses
in its reel of expressions
and we know her son

is off his meds again,
looking for gear in old haunts.

In our steamed-up kitchen,
my cards are always
weeping women, snowbound churches,
meetings on dark evenings
with whispered messages.

One birthday she gives me the cards
wrapped in black silk
torn from a blouse
and they fall behind my bed
among CDs, unread books.

Years pass and they vanish –
our futures stay wrapped in silk.
But the Fool still stands on my dresser;
a young man waltzing
towards a cliff-edge.

JESSICA TRAYNOR

THE BONNET

That Samhain we dressed as characters
    from *Persuasion*: we gender-bended
through the Finglas fields. I wore velvet
    trousers and cravat. You pranced about
in a bonnet we nicknamed Jane Austen:
    golden straw sprigged with silk columbine.

By the time we sat summer exams
    you were wasted. We read in your eyes
the opened grave, the funeral rain.

PAULA MEEHAN

LINING OUT

They were the big lads, the strong lads, the fit lads,
with their gum-shields and groin-guards, their county
    colour kit-bags;
we were the bozos in the hand-me-down sad rags,
alone in our windswept goalposts, looking on.

They were the boys with the thick-knit socks
and long-lace boots, calf muscles like rocks;
we were the castaways in castoff togs,
marooned in our windswept goalposts, just about clinging on.

They were the ones who made every squad,
up front in the bus, all fired up like Greek gods;
they were the named, the famed, the proclaimed and
    the cherished;

we were the slow ones, the 'Christ sake, would you go ons!',
the frozen half-dozen last to be chosen,
the nameless, shameless interchangeable no ones;
we were the AN Others at the end of the list.

Teenaged he-men descended from bears,
blood on their knees, mud in their hair,
they were the boys with the ice in their hearts and their veins;

we were the wasters, the dodgers, the slackers,
the double vest-wearers, the chocolate snack-packers,
the most likely to get the ball smack in the kisser and faint.

And then something happened, some fate struck a spark,
the wind changed direction, the bright sky went dark,
and the ball like a comet came down in our hands
and we held it –

And suddenly as one they rushed to our sides
in a flood of approval, a surge of pure pride,
to lift us up into the air on a tide of forgiveness;

and that sodden rectangle of tread-beaten grass
to the rear of the school – now the danger had passed –
was O'Moore Park or Croker itself and en masse
the 'they' and the 'we' were transformed, at long last, into 'us'.

PAT BORAN (b. 1963)

WITCHES

It was dark then.
We walked like witches through town,
out of the suburbs
into the unknown,
unknowing.

We were pure –
in our hearts, in our words,
in our deeds:
while the slow ash of innocence clung

to the cigarettes we smoked
behind the bicycle sheds.

We would all burn later.

As it was, we were fools,
unkissed by the light
bright smile of the sun,
only happy when sad,
aching for boys
who were mad, bad,
dangerous to know.

Some of whom were poets.

Some lived in the woods, singing
songs in the bandstand, hymns for the high altar
sung to a tree, a one-legged hill cloud.

Some were working-class heroes.

And we circled the lake
as our skirts dragged the ground
to draw a dull glitter
up through the dirty snow:
circles and circles completed, crow-black,
while the bell called the darkness down
over St. Stephen's Green.

The moon washed the roofs
as we flew around the city, or danced
around our shoulder bags
(Saturday night at the *Os).

We were senseless as stones, as the birds
in the sky,
only living to fly.

We would all come down.
Later.

ENDA COYLE-GREENE (b. 1954)

RAVE

coschleiteach ar chosán
damhsaímid abhaile
le breacadh an lae,
dúidín deiridh na hoíche
á roinnt eadrainn,
dall ar shuansiúlaithe na traenach
beocht an doird fós ar preabadh
i gceol ár gcuislí
is dúghealacha lána
ag lonrú sa cheithre shúil ar leathadh.

DOIREANN NÍ GHRÍOFA

RAVE

with highheels in our fists,
we turn feather-footed,
swaying over dawn pavements,
last night's last joint pinched
between us, oblivious

to sleepwalkers on the train,
with bass still thudding in our veins,
and black moons swelling in each gaze.

DOIREANN NÍ GHRÍOFA

CONFIDANTE

We'd have pints
enough between us
to crowd this small table
with their empty columns.
It's late enough
to say what we're thinking
as you do on nights
such as these. I start.
So what's the deal with you and...
And she says
Don't ask me.
Don't ask me what I know
you're going to ask.
And I understand
I've plunged up to my elbows
in a real messy question,
hauled it dripping
onto the table, left it
splattered among the glasses.
I know how an answer
can define things
or strip them bare
but it still stings
to go un-confided in,

to leave the answer
empty of any weight
and feel guilty for the question.
I want to know
if they went home
I want to know
if she loves him
I want to know
if he calls her
when it suits him.
And I wonder
if the hunger
of my knowing
is why
she doesn't say.

ERIN FORNOFF (b. 1982)

I'M ON FIRE

Her student housing single bed mattress
  held not quite enough room for both of us.

Quotation marks on the divided line
  with the base of her spine pressed against mine,

we lay trembling on the edge of a cliff,
  listening to music with the lights off.

Yearning to reach my hand into the dark
  and start a riot of Halloween sparks

but too timid to move a single muscle,
    I stayed rigid, bent at a right angle,

counting quavers, minims and semibreves
    then uncurled and made excuses to leave.

On the way home, I paused to catch my breath
    and watched lit windows offer silhouettes.

ROSS THOMPSON

TENT

Maurice has lost his virginity
in a tent, or so he claims, out beyond
the new hotel with a foreign girl
who happened to be hitching through.

When the jeering has at last died down,
most of us grin, kick at the earth
or stare into the middle distance, shy
of being the first to give himself away.

That evening, like tourists on a trail
to some historic battleground, we troop
all the way out, the full mile or more
to the now famous field where the girl is
long since gone, though yes there does appear
to be a faint impression in the grass:
rectangular, for all the world like a door
and big enough for a man to pass through.

PAT BORAN

THE GAELTACHT

At the very top of Errigal,
along with Mags O'Neill and Anne-Marie
and Fearghal Short and Deirdre Long,
there was Nadia Jane Gilgunn,
a wondrous blonde from Iúr Cinn Trá
with visible crimson bra straps
and a Lemon Fanta tongue.

And, against all odds, she was the one
who froze on the ridge of One Man's Pass.
There at the clouded pinnacle,
stricken by the magical,
by space, and possibility perhaps,
she turned, in tears, to gleaming quartz
as she straddled, gripped and clung.

JOHN KELLY

TREE HOUSE

The beech is all soar and space,
skin like an elephant, smooth as bed sheets.
It is the erasing of a tree among the pine's feral
cross-hatch, their crusts of bark.

Its arching grace caught us. We hauled boards
and nails as our morning bloomed plans.
Look at a beech long enough, you want
to run your hands up its trunk like a lover.

We laid over the crotch of its branches
a tongue and groove floor, a forest parquet
open to the sky, smooth enough to lay a cheek on.
Hammered low walls beneath canopy and clouds.

But a ballroom floor proves unfit for the elements.
Slowly black leaves clumped. The clouds brought rain.
Rain brought mould. The trunk pushed outwards as it
    thickened.

The whole operation crumpled, a receipt in a fist,
as the tree opened skyward and spread.
We had welcomed the weather, chosen no roof, denied
the inevitability of season and gravity. Grown up.

ERIN FORNOFF

PART THREE

"Henceforth I ask not good fortune – I myself am good fortune;
Henceforth I whimper no more, postpone no more, need nothing.
Strong and content, I travel the open road."
          —Walt Whitman, 'Song of the Open Road'

IN YOUR OWN DREAMTIME

Somewhere between creation and birth
in your own dreamtime
your journey outward began.
Before you ever saw the light of day, the sun rose, set on you
on three continents.
You crossed oceans once, twice, four times.
You ask *where* before *why*,
your fingers tracing a river on a map,
following the flow from source to sea.
Lines of latitude mark your space.
You reach to grasp poles, stretch toward the equator.
There's no holding you back.
I can see the open road in your eyes.

LYNN CALDWELL (b. 1963)

ARGENTINA

Two guys from Argentina
Talking away that first night,
I slept on a mattress on the floor

Unable to understand a thing;
Spain, a word come into its own
Like it or not, being there was stumbling

Into the wardrobe of another's dream.
I read the signs through the heat haze,
Instructions involved a street named

Calle de la República de Argentina,
Then Argentina won the World Cup;
I prized a living out of the livid city.

PATRICK KEHOE (b. 1956)

PANDA

My girlfriends are surrounded by silks
and I am outside,
looking in on this library of femininity:
rolls of ruby and cherry blossoms,
cool sapphire dragon pools,
jade envy forests –
manuals to be chosen from
just beyond the stall of heady spices,
in the Duyun covered market.

I shuffle softly to hide my girth
behind a butcher block table
while the seamstress giggles,
fingertips to lips,
at the numbers that measure
my friends' willowy western lengths.
Their souvenirs: handmade Chi Paus –
dresses cut slender, holding perfect
the memory of their figure
beloved in this welcoming space.

My souvenir: fear
of the tape wide
round my hips, my thighs,
my belly –
marking the size of
a true 'panda',
Chinese slang for 'westerner', or
the name of an animal
which is black-eyed, weary,
fumbling,
unapproached,
unnapproaching.

JENNIFER MATTHEWS (b. 1976)

RUE ST PAUL

I see them standing in the small room, the one I rented
for them on rue St Paul – Hôtel du Septième Art.
A couple from Ireland, in their fifties, in a hotel

on a street crammed with shabby-chic antique shops.
Do they look out of place? They had lived in London,
and in a provincial city, but their blood

was of the rural parishes of County Cork.
I'm older now than they were then.
In their unfashionable clothes and poor hair-cuts

they stand by the bed and marvel at the framed
black-and-white posters on the walls – Bogie, Bacall,
James Dean – as I outline my plans to shuttle them

between the Sacré Coeur and the Eiffel Tower, taking in
a *bateau-mouche* trip on the Seine, and they give
themselves up, willingly, to my banal tourism.

But my mother, menopausal, got up each morning at dawn
to walk the *quartier* in search of its wild cats. Maybe she met
the ghosts of animals from the zoo put there by a king.

And my father scrutinised the French racing pages,
trying to figure out the PMU betting system. He might
have got on well with the Portuguese migrants

who lived on the street in the fifties, when TB was rampant.
I stand there looking up at the boarded windows
of the cheap hotel, its fake Hollywood nostalgia

so at odds with the street's seventeenth-century houses
where the spectres of monks and merchants shuffle
between the roof beams. I see my parents

standing by the bed in the small room, desperate to
show me they understood what all the fuss was about.
I hope I was kind to them, but I doubt it.

MARY NOONAN (b. 1958)

REMNANTS

A long weekend spent sightseeing around Paris,
hammered after peach Bellinis from Aux Folies,
we wobbled from Sacre-Coeur to the Grand Palais,
Notre-Dame, the Louvre and the Musée d'Orsay

until we found a trapezium of indents
carved near where la Roquette no longer pressed against
the city skyline: five rectangles on the ground
where a guillotine, built by a German renowned

for making harpsichords, had once unencumbered
criminals of their skulls. The headless dead numbered
in the hundreds, and ghosts of traitors were revealed
all the way from the saltire to the breaking wheel.

I pictured your husband at your home in Quebec
and felt the crescent blade whispering on my neck.

ROSS THOMPSON

PASSOVER

I had no rest in my spirit … but taking my leave of them, I went from thence into Macedonia.
—Second Epistle to the Corinthians, 2:13

Because my land has water
more than wine
because my griefs were sheltered
from the wind
I made to travel
to the land of honey-blood
with mountains and a desert
and a trine of Gods
a river and a vineyard
and a host of tongues
a people and a highway
and a cusp of pasts.

I climbed Mount Korab in the sun
knelt at Saint Panteleimon

the heresy was to stand still
the trick was to move on.

BEN KEATINGE (b. 1973)

HEARING *THE BOATMAN'S CALL*
IN A BOSTON LAUNDROMAT

When I was 22, my day off was Tuesday,
and, come midday, I'd be ding-dinging through
the same grimy door on Massachusetts Avenue,

my hair piled high and loose, soft
jeans frayed, earlobes silver-hooped.
I was always dazed, thirsty, slightly stoned,

hip-hefting the same old basket
filled with the same old clothes.
I never had enough change, no,

I always had to feed another dollar to the coin machine,
before scooping dropped quarters up from the floor,
and spill-spooning detergent into the drawer.

Through that thin window, it all churned,
wet and muddled, but sometimes, I'd glimpse
a garment becoming itself if only for a moment –

the collar of a work-shirt's blue glance back,
or a jeans pocket kissing its cheek
against the glass. Next, they spiralled

damp to dry, all fly and fall and fall and fly,
while beyond the spool of walkman songs,
beyond *(Are You) The One That I've Been Waiting For?*

and *Where Do We Go Now But Nowhere*,
all I could see was washing machines,
as though many clock-faces had sprung open

to give a glimpse of cogs and springs,
all spinning, all whirring in foamy momentum,
every Tuesday afternoon, when I lived in the distance.

DOIREANN NÍ GHRÍOFA

WINTERING

That was my last year in Florida,
illegal and thinking of marriage
as one way to stay. Sleepless nights
of argument and indecision. And

to keep us going I worked a cash job
at an orchid farm. Long hours
in the sun, poor in paradise, the heat
on my back, drilling for a living.

I worked with a Mexican.
My man Victor, the orchid keeper
called him, friendly and amused
at the affluent couples who came

to purchase the rich, ornate dreams.
We buried a dead owl together.
I remember that. And my body
aching in the sun. Floating home to arguments.

What we were doing I was told
was wintering. Getting ready
for the cold, its indiscretion, its disregard.
Nailing sheets of plastic onto a wooden

frame, hammering, drilling,
to protect the fragile flowers
and their steel interiors, their
engineered hearts and worth.

That is already a long time ago.
Its contradictions apparent.

Wintering in sunshine. The past
still growing towards the light.

I think of them now as some sort
of emblem of that past, ghostly
orchids shedding their petals,
as we winter here ourselves,

batten down the hatches and wait
for whatever storm is coming, whatever
calamity the cold has to offer us
in the same way the orchids do,

I suppose, waiting through winter
to emerge with budding, fantastical
insistence, to wake and remind us:
be nothing less than amazed.

PAUL PERRY

FOOTFALL

Our shadows stretch ahead of us.
The cool November yellow
reminds us of Florian's feast day,
the way we can laugh at anything.
I carry her handbag, wonder at how
such a small vessel can weigh
so much, how such a small shoulder
can carry this much around,
footfall after footfall, and I promise
to take her to the first coffee shop

I can find after we call to the church,
check the notices and add our own –
looking for work, good English,
hardworking, optimistic. She kisses
this handwritten sheet for luck then pins it
to the board, leaving behind a piece of her
spirit; and we walk to the next source,
refill ourselves with held hands
and petrol station coffee.

The steam swirls between cold
and the next day of work, and we step
over that low wall, leave the forecourt,
laugh at the sight of a fully robed monk
who carries a sign for the last
pizzeria before Oughterard,
and we can't even pronounce
that place, but we laugh anyway,
that early morning tickle laugh that lasts
all day when the woman you love
is holding your hand and you can't see
past the length of your shadow
on a low-sun day in Galway in November,
when you can't see the long grey days
that will pull down the winter,
the way the rain will get everywhere
and black streets turn grey, slick
with rain, thinking you're strong
and can walk all day.

CELESTE AUGÉ (b. 1972)

WHILE BLEEDING

In a vintage boutique on Sullivan's Quay,
I lift a winter coat
with narrow bodice, neat lapels,
tight waist, a fallen hem.

It's far too expensive for me,
but the handwritten label [1915]
brings it to my chest in armfuls of red.

In that year, someone drew a blade
through a bolt of fabric and stitched this coat
into being. I carry it

to the dressing room, slip
my arms in; silk lining spills
against my skin. To clasp
the belt is to draw a slow breath
as a cramp curls again
where blood stirs and melts.

In glass, I am wrapped in old red –
        red pinched into girl cheeks
        and smeared from torn knees,
        lipstick blotted in tissue, scarlet
        concealed in pale sheets, all the red
        that fell into pads and rags –
the weight of red, the wait for red
that we share.
In the mirror, the coat blushes.

This pocket may once have sheltered
something precious: a necklace, a love letter,
or a fresh egg, feather-warm, held gently

so it couldn't crack, couldn't leak through seams,
so it couldn't stain the dress within.

DOIREANN NÍ GHRÍOFA

WHAT WOKE UP

I remember the night I didn't survive and what woke up
    the morning after wasn't me anymore
I can remember that wet July night I didn't survive and what
    woke up the morning after was different
I think I can remember one night I didn't survive and how
    something woke up instead of me the morning after
And a kiss on my skin
Yes, that kiss which burned my thin pale neck
But the metal kiss is still burning on my neck, connecting
    the dots
So am I still the one that
Woke up instead of me?
Woke up dead instead of me
Woke up screaming instead of me
What woke up the morning after is slowly forgetting the night
    I didn't survive.

POLINA COSGRAVE (b. 1988)

EXCURSION

Diminuendo of repeated forms,
tracks regressing to infinity
revive my panic dream of
a train that may or may not come.

On the nastiest
day of the year so far
I'm waiting at Dundalk Station
for the Belfast train back home

sitting on one of four pine chairs
around an oval table
in the Ladies' Waiting Room
where no Ladies wait

surrounded by monochrome
photos of railwaymen
the days when a body could go
from Greenore to Donegal

and full colour posters
with questions in four languages
aimed at other women
who must have travelled here in hope.

I answer in their absence
according to my circumstances.
As birth and class and
luck would have it

nyet, I am not a sex slave
nu, I am not being trafficked
non, I am not a victim
bu shi, I am not in fear.

ANN ZELL (b. 1933)

59

THE ROAD OUT

How was I to know the road out
would be the road back?
Home itself ephemeral –
found in the scent of boxwood,
a drift of cherry leaves,
the odd snowflake,
a hand to hold.

How was I to know you
would give the best directions,
your compass aligned to my true north?
Always ready
to go off road with me,
to make tracks where no one should go.

My own terrain is changed;
knowing the map of your body helps.
I have memorised lines and contours;
I could read it with my eyes closed.
You are good at reading the road,
always remembering the way back.

LYNN CALDWELL

ROOTED

Next to the stone threshold
she buried
the shrivelled umbilical cord.

An apple sapling marked the spot –
her offspring
close to home.

A lifetime away, in spring,
I ache, tugged by that string
back
to apple blossom
at the stone threshold.

VICTORIA MELKOVSKA (b. 1977)

32 KG SUITCASE

before I left home
I packed a 32 kg suitcase

I still have some
of the clothes and books
shoes and photographs
my grandmother's notes and coins collection
and memories from my first ever flight

the suitcase is still here
covered in dust

if I was to come back
what would I pack?

a red brick from henrietta street
a slang dictionary from the north inner city

burdock's fish and chips
bookshops: books upstairs and chapters
fragments of stories from smokers
huddled in doorways

but how can I go back
after leaving home
I became a stateless citizen
with a 32 kg suitcase

RAFAEL MENDES (b. 1993)

PART FOUR

"All life's grandeur
is something with a girl in summer"
—Robert Lowell, 'Waking Early Sunday Morning'

CHOICE

after Albert Camus

Give me solitude
or the perfect storm of love
nothing less will do.

GERRY MURPHY

VALENTINE

The girls are in their knickers again.
It's that time of year. There are hearts –
red, plush or sparkly – dangling in windows,
and teddy bears, and girls. Undressed.
It must be cold under the white lights
of the display. The yellow street lamps add
a sickly glow to the anemic bodies. They look

pinched, the thin girls in their frillies – pale
pink lace balcony bras and high-rise briefs
with touches of white satin. One girl
stares out, brazenly, a ring-leader of sorts.
She's the one who has graduated to wearing
scarlet and black, with sheer stockings and
suspender-belt. The works.

The new storms – Gertrude, Henry –
are blowing in from America, up-scuttling
bins, rivers. There are ice crystals in the
low-flying clouds, causing rainbow effects.
A child on his way home from school stops
to take in the hearts, the teddies, the scanties,
mesmerised by their magical affinities.
I stand there imagining what happens
at 4 a.m., when there's only a dim night-light
burning, and the *tableau vivant* starts to move.
The mannequins peel red tinfoil from heart-
shaped chocolates and scoff them, then lie
under heavy blankets dragged from the next
window and hold each other. Sleep.

MARY NOONAN

I WILL GABBLE

No matter my dream of you will not –
you rang, out of the blue I was tumbling about
moiling as usual the phone stopped me in my tracks
I had long since stopped believing in a world
that could take my breath away but there you were

phoning and asking to meet me for lunch
such a small thing, for me, a miracle, asking to meet
me, still shaking from the shock of seeing you
in the street after one of our eight-year intervals
the lop-sided smile, the mystifying eyes, the bulk
of you just one big question-mark I wanted to file away
under 'to cry about' and then you rang, caught me
on the turn in the stair, dogged in my belief in an earth
bent on its predictable axis, I in my runnel, pecking
and scratching for ever and instead I was picking up
the phone and there you were my heart ripped
from its coat of mail and tap-dancing all over my chest
and no matter I will gabble and you will look at me as
at something you couldn't make up and no matter
my dream of you will never – you rang.

MARY NOONAN

'A BOATMAN LOSES HIS OARS'

A boatman loses his oars
        at the mouth of the Yura –
he cannot know where
        he will end up. That's me –
caught in love's undertow

SONE NO YOSHITADA (late 10th century)
Translated from the Japanese by James Hadley and Nell Regan

IN IKEA

Here, doors lead nowhere. Daisy-print curtains open to concrete.
No spiders build webs, no dust falls. From a forest of frames,
the same strangers grin; soon they feel as familiar as cousins.
We find their belongings strewn around each fake room.
My feet are tired. I start to imagine myself as one of those
framed strangers – cardboard. We wander the floors,
bored burglars, lifting things and putting them back again.

My breath is hot. Come closer, let me whisper:
In my pocket I've hidden an assembly key. It will fit
every flimsy flat-pack here. It unlocks every slot.
I could dismantle all these doors and beds and floors.
We could watch it all fall.

You know, I could take you to pieces too,
I could slip this key between your collarbones,
your earlobes, your thighs. I could unlock all your sockets.
Come behind this cupboard. Open your buttons.
Let me unpack you.

DOIREANN NÍ GHRÍOFA

THE MAP

The map of my heart,
If you read it right,
Is full of canyons, sorrows,

Crows in autumn,
Lightings and ashes
Skylines blackening, growing clearer,

Leopards and horses
Hunted, starved,
An eagle vanishing into its sky,

A traveller's swampland, the love-cry
Of a bird at evening
Reaching you.

YAU NOI (b. 1965)
Translatled from the Chinese by Liu Xun and Harry Clifton

SWANS

I didn't know you'd followed me
the night I left the house

slammed, stormed

too drunk to drive
unable to get far enough away

pissed

You watched me walk to the canal
stand on the bridge

lingered

There were swans on the water
I was crying

wept

After a while I came back
hoping you'd ask for pardon

beg, implore

you wore a knowing smile
How were the swans? you asked

wryly, wrongfooting me,
transposing us to a minor key

where I could laugh again,
get off my high horse,
lay down my arms,

lay down.

KATHERINE DUFFY (b. 1962)

TOMORROW

"Sit down and I'll get us a couple of beers,
Here, borrow my hanky and dry your tears,
It'll all be the same in a hundred years
And things will be better tomorrow, my darling,
Things will be better tomorrow.

For the world each day is minted new,
And the sun is gold and the sky is blue,
And if that's a lie it's a good lie too
And things will be better tomorrow, my darling,
Things will be better tomorrow."

O silver the river and yellow the sand
And fair as a flower from a faraway land
Is the girl with her hand in his faithless hand.

TOM MATHEWS (b. 1952)

LABURNUM

You walk into an ordinary room
an ordinary evening, say
mid May, when the laburnum

hangs over the railings of the Square
and the city is lulled by eight o'clock
the traffic sparse, the air fresher.

You expect to find someone
waiting though now you live
alone. You've answered none

of your calls. The letters pile
up in the corner. The idea
persists that someone waits while

you turn the brass handle and knock
on the light. Gradually
the dark seeps into the room. You lock

out the night, scan a few books.
It's days since you ate.
The plants are dying – even the cactus,

shrivelled like an old scrotum
has given up the ghost. There's
a heel of wine in a magnum

you bought, when? The day
before? The day before that?
It's the only way

out. The cold sweats
begin. You knock back a few.
You've no clean clothes left.

He is gone. Say it.
Say it to yourself, to the room.
Say it loud enough to believe it.

You will live breath
by breath. The beat of your own heart
will scourge you. You'll wait

in vain, for he's gone from you.
And every night is a long
slide to the dawn you

wake to, terrified in your ordinary room
on an ordinary morning, say
mid May, say in the time of laburnum.

PAULA MEEHAN

STORM

I'm crushed, torn
from the wedding
photographs. You're

drenched with rain
and alcohol and women's
perfume. The fairytale

ended and for us there's
no tomorrow. The doves
flew away, their nest

ripped apart. It wasn't
strong enough to survive
the storm. They say

a home is built for two.

AGNIESZKA FILIPEK (b. 1982)

I AM THE WOMAN

I am the woman
you might ring again
when you're bored of television

I am the woman
you could invite again
if someone else cancelled

I am the woman
you wouldn't invite
to a wedding

I am the woman
you wouldn't ask
for a photo of her child

I am the woman
who isn't somebody's woman
for life.

ULLA HAHN (b. 1946)
Translated from the German by Anatoly Kudryavitsky & Yulia Kudryavitskaya

RANDOM CATALOGUING

On my bookshelves,
between Conrad's *Heart of Darkness*
and Saint Augustine's *City of God*,
a hand-book on Tantric Sex.
I can hear some of my ex-girlfriends
laughing out loud at this.

I can hear all of them.

GERRY MURPHY

'OTHER THAN YOU'

Other than you,
    cherry blossom, my
mountain love –
    there is no one
with whom I am intimate.

GYŌSON (1055–1135; former High Buddhist Priest)
Translated from the Japanese by James Hadley and Nell Regan

THE RING

We bought it in a pawn store
on Westheimer. We were already
married a year. You wanted
to wear it right away and not
wait on the charade I had planned.
You were right.
I wondered sometimes
whose ring it was before
it became ours, or yours,
how had it found its way
into the pawn store,
a small diamond,
among all the televisions,
video recorders, camcorders,
cameras, knives, jewellery,
pornography and guns.
Later, when it had all gone wrong,
when we had gone wrong,

when you had turned up without
the ring to take the furniture
that was yours, it was all yours,
I noticed the absence,
but said nothing. That night
I found the receipt
by the bedside table, no
note, just the ring's receipt
and I thought about it,
the ring, returned to where
it waited, to where it belonged.

PAUL PERRY

HAIR PIECE

When reading you used
catch, twist, lick
a strand of hair.

You'd place it gently
in your ear, until
it grew quite cold.

A circuit was completed,
a bright halo which
left me in the dark.

Now you've had your hair
cut short, your hands
flutter like moths

at the lamp of your ear.
I've made a ring
of hair.

It's a betrothal.
Try it for size.
It binds you to nothing.

MARK ROPER (b. 1951)

THE PLAN

On Malahide's light-washed beach
the young couple playing some strange game –
pacing back and forth with sticks and tape,
and not a ball in sight – turn out to be

mapping out the house they plan to build,
its walls and doorways inscribed in the wet sand,
moving from imagined room to room
beneath the setting sun, the rising moon.

PAT BORAN

HONEYMOON

Not the coast of Galicia, but the shores of Achill
in June, in honeymoon weather:
between sunshine and sunshowers
and the thunder you said was only the small gods
running across the island mountain.

From the heather beds of early summer
we dashed to the water, cold sand under heel –
you in that lemony garment of wool,
I in psychedelic shirt, not knowing which of us
was the lover and which the beloved.

GERARD SMYTH (b. 1951)

LOVE SONG

Remember when I came to you
clothed only in catastrophe?
You whispered, 'If I unbolt my heart,
you must walk through or walk away.'
Remember? And once inside, we coupled,
unlearned the sad refrain we once called loneliness.
We became the boat. Reefed our sails
in squally weather, sailed our course together.
When judgment fell
and the fleet railed 'recollect your family's
good name, *we're* your class remember',
you gave my tears to the sea and the sea
wept. They hauled our sheet
through the block, and when our boat luffed,
we corrected, we stemmed the line.
And after the wind arrived as a huge silence,
I asked if we could ever be becalmed
and you said no, we *have locked
ourselves inside one heart*, remember.

ELEANOR HOOKER (b. 1963)

PART FIVE

"I know a baby, such a baby,
    Round blue eyes and cheeks of pink"
—Christina Georgina Rossetti, 'I know a baby, such a baby'

GUEST IN REVERSE

You were the guest in reverse,
cluttering up the house
and making your presence
felt long before you arrived,
not to mention the bump.
We took delivery of
your changing table and lost
half of our living room,
capacious enough
to change a baby elephant.
Your clothes though
new, needed to be washed
in advance. I asked no questions,
and so babygrows fluttered
on the clothesline and were oddly
decorative in their premature
announcements. Socks in rainbow
stripes curled on the radiator.
One morning drinking tea

before work, I took one in my hand
and marvelled at the unimaginably
tiny foot that would come to fit it.
And in the cluttered cubby-hole
I had called my study, the door jammed
on a hastily secreted purchase,
a moulded plastic seat, safe for you
to sit in like a pharaoh being washed
in the great dry dock of the bath.

JOSEPH WOODS

FREE DIVE

The pelvic bones are parting like the Red Sea on Moses'
    command.
I know her eyes are open wide in the dark, lashes touch
    as she blinks.
When she dreams, I wonder what she dreams about.
Does anything else exist for her other than this nine-
    month-long free dive in the amniotic fluid?
Maybe she sees herself as a pearl hunter
fearlessly exploring the depths?
She collects the treasure and, on just a single breath,
    surfaces from the ocean floor!
Or maybe she stays underwater a little longer to play
    with the sparkling fish?
To find a secret cave full of skeletons and pirate coins!
There is something else, a note I left for her on the mossy wall:
Pain is a sign of life.

While the pelvic bones are parting like oyster shells to reveal
    the pearl,
My heart grows whole.

POLINA COSGRAVE

MÍREANNA MEARAÍ

Ar feadh i bhfad,
ní bhfuair mé ort ach spléachadh:
scáil a scaip
faoi chraiceann teann;
mo bholg mór
poncaithe ag pocléimneach –
gluaiseacht glúine nó uillinne,
cos, cromán nó mirlín murláin
sa mheascán mistéireach a d'iompair mé.

Le breacadh lae, phléasc tú
ón domhan dorcha sin,
is chaith mé míonna milse
ag cuimsiú píosaí do mhíreanna mearaí,
á gcur le chéile, á gcuimilt:
Trácht coise i mbos mo lámh,
cuar cloiginn i mbaic mo mhuiníl.

Chuir mé aithne mhall ort, a strainséirín.

DOIREANN NÍ GHRÍOFA

JIGSAW

For months,
there was little I could glimpse
in your jumble of limbs, but a muddle
of shadows stirring under my skin.
Untranslatable: my swollen middle
suddenly punctuated by the nudge
of knee or ankle, perhaps a small
knuckle rolling past fast as a marble,
maybe the cryptic twist of a heel or hip,

but once dawn drew you
from that dark world,
I spent months piecing
this jigsaw together at last, I saw
how the arch of your foot fit the hollow
of my palm, how your head nestled
into the curve of my neck. I knew it: we fit.

Then you grew, little stranger, and I grew to know you.

DOIREANN NÍ GHRÍOFA

THREADING THE LIGHT

It took thirty-six hours to bring you home
though it may have been more, and it may have been less;
a day and a half in the eye of the storm
of laughing gas and sheets scented with lemon zest.

Something was wrong from the off: a lost wedding ring,
a snippety shift nurse, several botched
epidurals and an afternoon spent watching
your stuttering heartbeat playing hopscotch

on a fuzzy screen. I split my time between
fetching naff sandwiches from the hospital canteen
and telling your mum everything would be alright
when I all I wanted to do was thread first light

into your eyes, and slap first breath into your chest,
but the timing was so tight, and the space in the cleft
so slight that I nearly forgot, and I nearly lost faith
but nothing is ever truly lost; it is only misplaced.

ROSS THOMPSON

YOU WERE BORN IN AN ARK

and the animals were as many as you could name
while waves chopped below
and we swayed with the winds.
All the while you slept as though
the rocking were internal, warm,
and you smiled inside.
Below animals stood to protect
us from the sea; and we were so safe
under the balsa bow,
the stern ahead, when Noah
cocked his head to see.
And when his dove flew in
we rejoiced – you felt
a kind of surge, like running,

but so still, and your mother smiled.
I loved the animals, erect, noble –
protected by their flesh;
they would have died for you.
When the ship docked
you were a tiny red thing;
we kissed you on the head
and started again

CHRISTIAN WETHERED (b.1987)

ATLAS

Unlike some of your friends
who were born with Down syndrome,
you had no bowels to be stitched,
no heart needing repair, no intestinal blockages.
You were my lucky Lily
but then icicles dripped in the spring thaw.

First, tiny tear ducts syringed.
Second, a grommet inserted in minuscule ear.
Third, tear ducts syringed, again.
Forth, tonsils and adenoids removed.
Fifth, another grommet for each faintly finer ear.

Five times they stuck in the cannula,
dressed you in a tiny gown with teddies.
Five times I sang to you while the anaesthetist
put mask over heart-shaped lips.
Five times you went limp,
disappeared behind sterile doors.

Five times I shuffled down the hall
tried to read, write. Stand. Sit.
Questioned my faith then prayed.
Minutes gonged. Thirty-five, forty-two
"She's not quite awake."
Forty six, forty seven, forty eight.

Then you gave a groggy smile.
I stroked your baby body,
cooed at my broken bird.
A nurse stood by you while I ran
down three flights of stairs,
inserted eight warm coins into filthy phone
told my mother in Alaska
"Lily's fine, just fine, fine."
Me too, I lied.

I wanted the icicle to stop dripping
so we could shut the hospital door
make friends with people who were not doctors
find someone who could hold up half the sky,
just once.

MARY MULLEN (b.1952)

SÓLÁS

(Nóta: Den Bhéaloideas é go bhfillfeadh anam an linbh mhairbh i riocht
an cheolaire chíbe is go dtabharfadh a ceol faoiseamh croí don mháthair)

Faoi cheo gealaí mean oíche,
de cheol caillte,
filleann sí ó chríocha ciana:
Aithním do bhall broinne,

a cheolaire chíbre
agus is fada liom go bhfillfidh tú arís
chugam.

DOIREANN NÍ GHRÍOFA

SOLACE

> *(Note: In Irish folklore, souls of dead infants were believed to*
> *return as sedge-warblers to comfort their mothers with song)*

Listen: in midnight
moon-mist, in snatches of lost music,
I've heard her return from the distance.
Little visitor, your birthmark looks so familiar.
Small warbler, listen, every night, I'll wait,
awake, facing north, until the last star-light fades.
Find me, child; I yearn for your return.

DOIREANN NÍ GHRÍOFA

Translated from the Irish by the poet

TAISÍ

In airde, i scórnach ghlas
i gcéislíní an chnoic
dreapaim ar nós damhán alla
go dtagaim ar scoilt, uaimhín.

Sáim mo cheann isteach:
taisíocht, caonach
boladh lofa-mhilis.

Bhíos anso cheana
gach fearsaid díom
caol fada órbhuí
luisne na hóige orm.

Cromaim isteach sa scairt.
Aimsím an mionchúil
taobh thiar de chlochdhoras
crochta ann fadó.

Leoithne tríd an uaimh
bogaim an dingchloch
is láimhseálaim cochall meannleathair
fillte thar chnámha is craiceann.

Ar bhos mo láimhe clé
m'iníon – anáil aon lae
diúltaithe di ag na déithe.
Mearbhall ar mo chroí

am na caillúna úd, uair
a shíneas géag éagmaiseach
síos faill is thána ar ubh
a sciobas ó nead.

Is mar san a fuaireas
m'iníon tacair a chaitheann a saol
im theannta gan eitilt
tochas aici de shíor ina guaillí.

Uaigneas orm go fóill, athshínim
mo lámh fhada síos an fhaill
go leagaim taisí an té a d'eitil
ar an seana-nead folamh.

CEAITÍ NÍ BHEILDIÚIN (b. 1958)

REMAINS

High up, deep in the green
throat of the hill
I angle spiderlike until I find
the opening, the tiny cave.

I put my head inside:
dankness, moss
sweet-smelling decay.

I was here before,
my long
bronzed, slender limbs
glowing with youth.

I bend low into the fissure.
I find the small niche
behind a stone door
fixed there years ago.

A breeze enters the cave.
I move the wedge-stone
and lift a soft leather mantle
enclosing bone and skin.

On the palm of my left hand
is my daughter – even a day's breath
denied her by the gods.
My heart astray

at the time of that loss,
I stretched a yearning limb

down a cliff and found an egg
I stole from the nest.

And so I came across
my foundling daughter who lives
flightless with me
her shoulders eternally restless.

Still forlorn, once more I stretch
my long arm down the cliff
and lay the remains of the one who flew
in the old, empty nest.

CEAITÍ NÍ BHEILDIÚIN
Translated from the Irish by Paddy Bushe

CHILD BURIAL

I chose your grave clothes with care,
your favourite stripey shirt,

your blue cotton trousers.
They smelt of woodsmoke, of October,

your own smell there too.
I chose a gansy of handspun wool,

warm and fleecy for you. It is
so cold down in the dark.

No light can reach you and teach you
the paths of wild birds,

the names of flowers,
the fishes, the creatures.

Ignorant you must remain
of the sun and its work,

my lamb, my calf, my eaglet,
my cub, my kid, my nestling,

my suckling, my colt. I would spin
time back, take you again

within my womb, your amniotic lair,
and further spin you back

through nine waxing months
to the split seeding moment

you chose to be made flesh,
word within me.

I'd cancel the love feast
the hot night of your making.

I would travel alone
to a quiet mossy place,

you would spill from me into the earth
drop by bright red drop.

PAULA MEEHAN

FIRELIGHT

I'd light the fire without meaning to,
I'd light it without noticing,
kindling and coal using my hands
to combust on the very warmest of days.

You in the light green chair, me
in the dark green, we'd sit, fire
flowering between us, its black nightgowns
slipping to the floor. Already

memorable, the coal we burn
re-deposited within us,
mine of ripeness, seam of grace.
Where unknown others sat before

and unknown others will again
we'd take our time. Fire privy
to our intimacies, fire privy
to the unspoken questions:

What is the price of seclusion?
What have we missed, being childless?
Its mild blast on our skin always
a reminder, a hint of a darkness

burnt into human skin in suburbs far
from an explosion. Mask of Hiroshima,
shadow scorched into all our flesh.
Good servant, bad master, fire insists.

Last thing we'd lie awake and watch
dying flames infiltrate the bedroom
and dapple the walls. We'd hear
the soft toc as clinker hit the pan.

A sudden flare might send me stumbling
to check all was well. I'd hurry back,
sobered, in violation
of a privacy. To see the fire gently

collapsing, talking to itself, heating
empty chairs, was to know what
the world would look like when
we're not there. Was to be thin air.

MARK ROPER

PART SIX

"I cannot remember that
instant when I gave my life to them
the way someone will suddenly give their life over to God"
—Sharon Olds, 'That Moment'

SCOOTER

Between our sure steps you pick your way
slowly at first, one foot ticking on the path,
the other planted on your new scooter.

Quickly, unexpectedly,
you stutter into your stride
till you are gliding, feet together,
just ahead.

While we exchange shy smiles of pride
you are suddenly farther on,
heartshockingly small beside the open road,
a skater on cracked ice
where big children knife by on bicycles.

There's a flashback to that first crawl
when the house bulged with dangers:
The fireplace a bludgeon for your head,

the table corner a spike for your eye,
the kitchen a nerve centre of poisons and avalanches.

Now we gasp into a run
at your heedless happiness
as you round the corner,
as we round the corner,
watching the gap widening.

CATHERINE ANN CULLEN

LET'S DIE

"Let's die," I say to my kids,
  Lee aged five, Luca not yet three,
  and under an August blanket of sun
  we stretch out in the grass on a hill
  to listen to the sea just below
  drawing close, pulling back,
  or to the sheep all around us
  crunching their way down towards earth.

"Do you love the clouds, Dada?"
"Do you love the Pink Panther?"
  and "Will you stay with us forever?"
  to which I reply, without hesitation,
  Yes, Yes and Yes again,
  knowing that as long as we lie here
  everything is possible, that any of the paths
  up ahead might lead us anywhere
  but still, just in time, back home.

Like me, sometimes they act too much,
filling the available space and time
with fuss and noise and argument,
but up here, overlooking the landscape,
the seascape, of their lives, on this hill
they like to play this game, to lie
together and together to die

which, in their children's language, means
less to expire or to cease
than to switch to Super Attention Mode,
to prepare for travel, to strap oneself
into the booster seat and wait and wait
for the gradual but inexorable lift
up and off and out into motion.

For my two boys, things are only
recently made flesh, made mortal –
our uprooted palm tree, two goldfish,
the bird a neighbour's cat brought down
last week – and they are almost holy
with this knowledge. "Let's die now,
then let's go home for tea," Lee says,
putting into words as best he can
the sea's helpless love affair with the land.

PAT BORAN

NIGHT BEFORE SCHOOL

It had rained all day, driving round Inverin and Moycullen
the landscape smudged like a child's painting,
the road a wet blackboard.

You slept most of the way home to Dublin,
your longest nap since you curled in a sling
just the other side of my womb.

I was the one stir crazy,
knowing what was ahead of you:
Hemmed into a uniform, a small desk and chair,
the compulsory sitting, your ceaseless chatter stifled.

And then the sun blessed us with a last kick of summer,
our small garden golden and glittering with drops,
the apples growing fairytale red.

We postponed dinner for Poddle Park.
You pedaled an heirloom bike through the slanting light
and I walked behind, drinking you in,
seeing how summer had grown you.

In my shadow, I'm a big girl, you laughed,
and the late sun flung a long figure on a high nelly
stretching away from us
over the shaking grass.

CATHERINE ANN CULLEN

LEICTREACHAS STATACH

Scaoilim leo i m'ainneoin féin.

Ag geata na scoile, ligim le mo ghreim
ar na lámha go drogallach, agus nuair a fheicim
an lasadh ina ngruanna, ní bhrúim póg orthu.
Imíonn siad trí na doirse gan breathnú siar.

Fillim abhaile i m'aonar agus tagaim orthu
sa triomadóir éadaigh, a ngéaga snaidhmthe
ina chéile, fite fuaite leis an leictreachas statach,
a gcuid léinte fillte i mbaclainn mo gheansaí,
fáiscthe le m'ucht.

Nuair a dhéanaim iarracht na héadaí a scaradh,
léimeann siad ina chéile le spréachadh aibhléise,

cúbann siar uaim de gheit.

DOIREANN NÍ GHRÍOFA

STATIC ELECTRICTIY

I let them go, in spite of myself.

At the school gate, I release my grip on their hands
with reluctance. When I notice their cheeks growing
blush-lit, I bite back my kisses. They stroll through
the doors without glancing over their shoulders.

I walk home alone and find them
in the dryer, their limbs twisted
into each other, gripped with static electricity,
their shirts tucked between my sweater sleeves,
pressed to my breast.

When I attempt to pull those clothes apart, they cling
to each other, firing electric sparks that startle me back,

flaring a static shock to fling me off.

DOIREANN NÍ GHRÍOFA

COCOON

Seeing the light leak from the crack under his bedroom door,
I hold my breath and tiptoe over the threshold.

Through the day's debris, my feet search for floor,
between piles of plastic dinosaurs, comics, tilting Lego towers.

A light shines from elsewhere – there –
the tented sheet. Underneath a torch glows.

I stand outside.   Apart.

The dark makes a mirror of his window tonight.
I see my reflection there – brown moth, drawn to his light.

DOIREANN NÍ GHRÍOFA

THE LONE PARENT DOES NOT WRITE

Between a bad back
and a deadweight Hoover
it's been a month or more.
Let's not talk about the duvet cover
walking out of the bedroom
in search of a good home.
At the sink I'm breeding botulism –
a resistance experiment.
Results are good,
besides, my kids have more brains
than to get sick; if their mother
stopped this frantic whirl
to tend a fevered brow,
she'd keel over, replace them in the bed.

This morning allows
I find our rooms again,
vacuum the top of rugs at least,
nothing too fancy,
nothing extreme.
This way I'm left
a tiny sacred hour,
to climb the laundry mountain
to part the sea of toys
and walk through,
the Egyptians at my back,
to sit,
just for one hour, here
in the Holy Land.

GRACE WELLS

MY MOTHER'S GETAWAY

'Aren't we lucky to have them?'
She meant the walking places,
her own wildering realm. No meals
to cook, no groceries to fetch,
no cows to milk, no cattle to herd
or sheep to flock. Danger?
There were only shallow drains
and slack fences to step,
with a hitch of her skirt, across.
Yes, 'across' – depend on her
to say that word. She'd go across
the Callows, face Aughty's
distant blue hills forecasting
fine weather, or face near-at-hand
Aughty's glum readiness
to add to the splosh of rust-red
ferric iron water in the field
known as Old Tillage. No walls
or trees for 'a quare hawk'
to hide behind, the land flat, her eyes
able to see far. She'd go
morning or evening to the nurture
of not thinking, her feet swishing
through coarse meadow –
go across, away from child and beast
and man, go beyond concern.

PATRICK DEELEY

A WOMAN OF ANGLO-IRELAND

My husband left me without a word,
without a penny. To raise our daughter
I worked nights in a bar, high and dry
in a welter of loosened tongues.

We lived by the river. Its lights
furnished our home. At summer's end
we gathered teazles and made them
into toys for sale in town.

I thought we were happy
but she left when she reached sixteen.
I fastened the boreen leaves behind her,
let the river be my only road.

It brings me wood, fattens mussels,
removes my small leavings. I love
its moist kiss in my lungs,
its silver hands between my legs.

You might think I can't cope.
Briars fillet the roof, books rot,
grease thickens, nothing works.

But I stood on the shore with four
dog foxes in a cathedral of moonlight
and they were not afraid of me.

MARK ROPER

EX-VOTO

Jasmine budding into flower, oranges
ripening, we had our first foreign holiday.

It was all beginnings and endings,
last responsibilities, new freedom.

Olivia so drunk she fell
off the curb into traffic.

Holly's neck purpled with love-bites
from a Cuban boy she met on a bus.

I was so surrounded by teenagers
I became one of them,

thinking of little more than mojitos,
ice and mint and sugar.

Mornings I was alone, in palaces and galleries,
and the archaeological museum

where I fell in love
with a wall of votive offerings,

Roman footprints carved in stone
and the simple lettering: ex voto.

Ex voto, my darlings,
for the journey and return.

GRACE WELLS

THE CHILDREN OF ALCOHOLICS

The children of alcoholics
make fine actors,
in broken homes, hurting homes,
learning from an early age
to deceive, to deflect
attention, when all else fails
to put a brave face on.

Look now, here they come,
the bright, the bold, the beautiful.
They kiss the air when they meet,
they stand upright and proud,
in darkness, speaking calmly,
confidently to the gods,
then bow and close their eyes
to vanish, if only for a moment,
in the wave-wash of applause.

And they need our love so much,
these hurting creatures,
that, somehow, sensing it,
we laugh and cry along with them,
freeing smaller hurts inside ourselves,
our applause and our tears –
if only they could be bottled –
as precious, as potent,
as addictive as alcohol.

PAT BORAN

A MOTHER MOURNS
HER HEROIN-ADDICTED DAUGHTER

How could I have dreamt
that my bird of paradise,
my green-clad hippie girl,
could be so reduced
to the gammon face of poverty,
the incessant whinge of a child.

If we rolled up time like a ball
I'd give you the cherries of my nipples,
I'd wash you almond clean
and lay your hair like lint
on the cartilage of my breast.

A prey to the barren street, you're lost
on the breach of years that no silk
nor cotton drawing-to of threads
can mend. The void. Your path is marked
like gull-prints on an empty beach.

The drug has perished your will.
You float like a stick on a pond
in here, in there – to a harbour of lily-trees,
or held for days in scum till the light
breeze lifts you and you edge along.

Will you walk on my street once more?
I'll raise my pavements to keep you safe,
open the balcony of my arms.
I will buckle your shoes again
and shine the mirror for your dance.

But you will not throw away your bag of tricks.
Your monkey fingers cling to the safety net
in which you nightly land, having walked
the trembling wire and heard the screams
of anticipation, seen the up-turned mouths.

How can we meet down the glaciers
of days, the furnaces of nights?

LELAND BARDWELL (1922 – 2016)

AEGIS

Offering is given at the end in thanks, and the maze that led
to the antique shop in Venice's ghetto was a pilgrimage of
　　twenty years.

Two rough decades – if there wasn't drama, there was crisis,
perpetual worry, a surfeit of strife. But not alone for love

is the heart made, and you children gave me courage –
a near invisible presence more like absence

until I saw it manifest in the antique-shop window, pinned
among small metal limbs – the aegis of two silver breasts.

All through your childhood I had leaned into their curve.
Now that you are leaving home, there comes a natural tally –

so many things I failed to provide, but the ex-voto breastplate
upholds, reassures me there was always milk.

GRACE WELLS

THE NEST

The building of it took place right under our noses,
in the hedge that bordered our lives just off our porch.
So at first we missed it, busy about our own
arrivals and departures, till the nest was good to go:
a springy wicker hold-all fitted into the notch
where branches diverged like the ribs of a vaulted arch
in a chapel that sways with all breezes
that blow, gets soaked in every rain.

Those cardinals with their blurred red
flourishes, scarlet avatars of pure instinct
coming and going with twigs in their beaks. Next
three eggs, and the female brooding on her nest
like a feathery smooth boat at drydock,
like a china hen in a farmhouse kitchen.
Then three crowded skyward mouths, pure need,
three dowdy tulips gaping toward the sun.

But a day came when they were gone for good
and we were not around to see –
after weeks when they were the talk of our household:
nest built, eggs laid, chicks hatched and flown
past the porch and trellis and into the open sky,
leaving the two of us here on our own,
peering down into their derelict oval.
I never saw anything so empty.

RICHARD TILLINGHAST (b. 1940)

A SAPLING BIRCH

You have grown out of our reach:
a seed sown long ago now
tall as this sapling birch. I
measure the infinite distance:
fingers of wind in the leaves like
my hands in your hair; a misty
April dawn resonant with bird-
song; our bedroom and the stranger
we welcomed there. So much you
owe to love's climate of kiss
and touch, the soil that nourished you,
the embracing light: remember this.
I hand you over to your lover now
to grow a seedling out of that good earth.
Grow it, grow it and let us rejoice
that you have grown out of our reach.
Out of the good earth grow a sapling birch.

FRANCIS HARVEY (1925 – 2014)

PART SEVEN

AND SUDDENLY YOU'RE AT THAT PLACE

where trees spread leafless fingers
trying to catch the low-slung, reckless sun.

You haven't time to grapple with the summer-
dust, the scratched CDs and tissue mice

for the ice of your dark glasses; instead,
you rack the music up, find notes

dropped sharp as sherbet on your tongue,
and you're back in your life, life going on.

ENDA COYLE-GREENE

AFTER OPHELIA

It is a Monday night in mid-October in the middle of my life
& there are trees down across Belfast & my bin has blown over
& sent the concrete block on top of it flying through the air
& the lads over the back fence are celebrating the fact
that we still have electricity by hosting a very loud disco
complete with multi-coloured flashing lights & so I am
    standing
outside on my back deck in my white plastic clogs slipping
on algae & patting my holly tree & looking up
at white clouds dancing across the sky in the post-hurricane
    winds
when Reach for the Stars comes over the fence till someone
    shouts
to put something else on & then the night is full of Polar
(Ripperton Remix) by Vök & there is nothing to be done but
join in.

EMMA MUST (b. 1966)

TOMORROW

Tomorrow
a different smell than usual
tomorrow
cyclamens are blooming in pink
tomorrow
we will drink radioactive water rained from heaven
tomorrow
even when the earth quakes, gets cold, then freezes

tomorrow

we will still be alive

tomorrow

even if the coagulated terror makes a bottomless cask of us

tomorrow

on the quaking and splitting earth

tomorrow

like flowers we will suck up poison from the soil

tomorrow

even if everything is lost

tomorrow

tulips will let their muddy green leaves bulge

tomorrow

and open their buds all at once in red, yellow and white

tomorrow

with a smile on our faces we will live

tomorrow

wishing to meet someone somewhere

tomorrow

we will plant sunflower seeds

tomorrow

open the curtains on the window as usual

tomorrow

to fill the room with sunshine

tomorrow

we will live on the earth as usual

tomorrow

when we wake

tomorrow

MIKIRO SASAKI (b. 1947)
Translated from the Japanese by Beverley Curran and Mitsuko Ohno

GOING TO THE WELL

'Everyone,' he said, 'should have their own well.'
Those words of wisdom, fresh as sun-dried hay,
hit home to us, as we crossed hill after hill

of bogland. Guided down to the bottom of a hill,
we found a well, and as the wooden lid was lifted,
a shallow body of turf-coloured water trembled.

It reminded me of an old abandoned well
in my own backyard far away;
long sealed-up, its water stained with oil.

When I go home, I should clean that well.
Or, first, find and clean the well in me.
The fallen leaves covering up my well

back home are nothing compared to the well
of apathy long stored-up and nursed in me.
Here the water, drawn fresh from the well

and stored in a clay kitchen pot, settled.
Sharp and clear as the blue patch of sky
peeking through a hole in the clouds, it thrilled

my tongue and throat. Everyone should have a well.

MUTSUO TAKAHASHI (b. 1937)
Translated from the Japanese by Mitsuo Ohno & Frank Sewell

A MEETING IN NAJU'S BAR

20-years-older-I sent me a letter proposing to meet.
I replied that I would bring along 20-years-younger-I.
So, we met.
The old hostess Naju was still serving drinks and eatables.
Roasting pork belly on the briquette stove,
Past-I drank red-labeled soju,
I drank millet wine, and
Future-I's nerves had weakened from too much drink
So he sipped bean sprout soup.

We all laid our memories out on the table.
We agreed to keep our wife and children out of it.
Though we all suspected one another's differences,
We comforted each other with our ability to forget.
Past-I said he was reading Karl Marx,
I said I was reading travel books, and
Future-I said he didn't read books any longer.
Our talking started obscurely.

During our talk, the grill pan was changed twice,
The wine cups were shuffled,
And the now-cool bean sprout soup was reheated.
I asked them about their happiest moments.
Past-I said that there were no happy moments, only sad ones.
Future-I managed to top his cynicism, saying
That present is always the abyss into which
Past and future are swallowed –
It makes life happen whether or not we want it to,
And forces a bare survival in life's toil.
At that moment, somebody overturned the table in anger.

Looking back,
I have tried to piece together my shattered memory of those
    three hours,
Past-I shouted out "do we even know the difference
    between 'truth' and 'fact'?"
I spoke ill of Lee, my department head, as 'Rascal', and
Future-I kept talking about mother who had passed away
    long ago.
I remember the hostess Naju pushing our backs out of the bar,
But I can't remember how we parted ways.
Like in a dream, somebody seemed to say
"Bastard!" That was the last thing I remember.

HANYONG JEONG (b. 1958)
Translated from the Korean by the Seth Feldman

WEEKEND AWAY

The car slows for the turn,
for the ring-rumble
of a cattle grid.
Wheels greet gravel
and we're here.

We love this blessed threshold,
our hidden compound
with fossils in the doorstep,
where fishermen sip whiskey
and chat about the day:

Oh, he's a hard man on the rods.
Oh, Jesus, he's a hard man on the rods.
Goes for distance. He belts it out.

And oh, that echo on the wooden boards
as we head up to the room.
The big clattering key.
The cool sheets. The furnishings.
Our own invisibility.

We can run a bath.
Or run amok. Or both.
Or sit downstairs, for now,
and read our books. Hear the anglers'
talk of Silver Stoats and Gorgeous George

and how to gink him up.
Chowder and a pint perhaps.
Or look at maps of Derryclare and Maam.
Perhaps the mountains? Or an ice-cold swim?
It seems, love, that we can still do anything.

JOHN KELLY

AFTER THE HOLIDAY

After the holiday
we drive home, check the house,
walk into the garden.

After the dark red desert,
after all those animals and birds,
I feared it might disappoint.

After all the bright talk
with our friends, I feared
we might be lonely.

We listen to the stream,
its two notes. A robin
taps out its take on things.

The apples are ripening.
The wild ginger's in flower.
Slowly the known air

begins to unclothe us.
Across the field the horses
make their shy approach,

like our lives, coming back.

MARK ROPER

INTRUDER

He doesn't recognize me, this scrawny kid
a few summers back still mowing lawns
for pocket money, now suddenly reborn
as the local tearaway, his shaved head
exposed in the full-moon beam of my flashlight
to the rear of the house, the world fast asleep,
autumn yet, by a thread, by the skin of its teeth.

"Looking for my ball," he says, matter of fact,
defiant, in his hand, half on show,
a bat or something heavier proposing
the alternatives. "At this hour?" I laugh
and stand my ground, part fool, part sage,

wondering what else might lie within reach
in the inky dark that floods the moment's page.

He sniffs, shifts uneasily, never looks away.
It's as though he's faced me a dozen times before,
the drunken father staggering through the door
at closing time, fists raised, shouting obscenities
for the whole estate to hear. Silence. A grunt,
then he's over the six-foot wall in a judder
of branches and shadows, less like a creature

fleeing than a creature in flight, the night air
electric, the garden alert to the brim
of the fence posts, the cap-stones, the tendrils of clematis
inching up through the stars ...
                              In the flickering dark
I wait for the echo of footsteps retreating,
hear nothing at all. Instead, like a picture
taken from orbit, there's us here, this youngster
and my middle-aged self, two figures bent double,
catching our breaths, one stood in grass
neatly trimmed, the other in splinters of glass
from a dangling street-lamp, hearts pumping
faster than lovers', the wall here between us
ungiving (yes), alien (surely), and cold to the touch –
not living (of course) and yet somehow
bristling with gooseflesh.

PAT BORAN

IN OUR STAIRWELL

In the evenings,
a bunch of youths
dwelt in our stairwell.
They drank vodka,
pissed up the wall
and jeered humankind.
Every morning, as I went to work,
there was an empty bottle
on a landing,
and it smelt of urine.

Once I said to the youngsters,
'You may drink vodka if you wish,
but it would be better if you
refrained from urinating here,
it's not a nice thing to do.
As for humankind,
we should not laugh at it
but mourn it.'

Since that day
the youths in our stairwell
drink vodka,
lament bitterly over humankind
and exhaust themselves
abstaining from urination.
They would rather die than take a piss.

GENNADY ALEXEYEV (1932 – 1987)
Translated from the Russian by Anatoly Kudryavitsky

NIGHT START

Sleep easy, love, the day will come around
And light the glass, and warm the windowsill.
Lie close, lie still, you only dreamt that sound.

Forget you heard the snarling of the hound,
The harsh breath, the snap that almost killed
Sleep. Easy, love. The day will come around.

That wail is not the voices of the drowned,
But the salt wind beating up the hill.
Lie close, lie still. You only dreamt that sound.

And that was not a tremor of the ground,
Just my arm shivering in a sudden chill.
Sleep easy. Love. The day will come around.

I conjure past and future to surround
This night, this room, to witness that we still
Lie close. Lie still, you only dreamt that sound.

So rest, my love, assured. What we have found
Settles around us, an earnest that we will
Sleep easy. Love, the day will come around.
Lie close. Lie still. We only dreamt that sound.

PADDY BUSHE (b. 1948)

GRAVITY

We all come
through the gate into your field
and so gently
you keep us in place we forget,
your touch unfelt.

Each day your weight takes
an inch, each night
we rise slowly back to size.
Pressed down
our heads open up to heavens.

When I fell I knew
this was not a fall, it was you
taking hold of me,
speeding me, rolling me over,
I felt your grab

for the first time, push or pull
I don't know which,
in those split seconds it seemed
that mountain,
very earth and sky had turned

against me, were
beating me up – but it was only
your ancient will,
doing what it does, making
light of everything.

MARK ROPER

POSTCARD FROM HOSPITAL

Just a few post-observation lines to say
Your diagnosis was spot-on. All samples,
Syringes, charts and consultants now confirm
The diabetes you nagged so patiently about.

So this is just to thank you, and your blood's
Worth bottling too. Forgive the sour words.
All I could hear was a threatening buzz
And, shying from imagined stings,

I slapped uselessly at myself, forgot
The rich slow dripping in the comb.
Now I must find a new path to the hive
And savour every taste along the way.

I'll be home soon, complete with my prognosis,
Craving mouth upon mouthful of your sweetness.

PADDY BUSHE

RED MOUSE

You ask for your navy ink pen,
your notebook – oh, and the red mouse.

I imagine it, nestling in the pages
of the spiral-bound notebook,

see it now nibbling its way
through scribbles thin as its tail

breakfasting on troubadour songs
or dialogues from your play.

But I find instead a red plastic device
snug in the palm of my hand,

small enough to wrap amongst your
clothes, the hospital corridor white

and endless as an airport's,
though there is no plane to catch –

only you, resting behind curtains, marking
words on a screen, the red mouse sliding

over the pale blue blankets of the ward,
your fingers deleting illness with a click.

ENDA WYLEY

VISITING THE LOCKED WARD

Lights waltz like petals in her waterjug,
Watching which random choreography
She says, 'They talk about me. Later on
The birds will corkscrew out of the night like that.'

Penguin Beckett, packet of sanitary towels
Caught in the pulsing violet ambulance light.

'Love,' she says, 'is a mouse in a forest of owls
And I burn in the morning before I am delivered.'

And I burn in the morning.

TOM MATHEWS

'SUCH A LIFE THEY THINK'

Such a life they think
    I live! As if my retreat
on Mount Uji,
    south east of this city,
could shelter me from grief.

KISEN (Mid 9th century; Buddhist Master)
Translated from the Japanese by James Hadley and Nell Regan

ESTUARY

'Soon there will be no birds left at all,'
says the elderly man on the bench
overlooking the estuary where a dozen curlews
bend to stitch the frayed edge of blue silk.
It has been so calm, so still all day.
Maybe he is my myth visitor,
come to impart some unwanted darker news.
I sit beside him. Whatever he has read
is already haunting him, the ink
on his fingertips. We talk for hours,

until, silver-grey, the evening tide slips in
around our feet. Tonight I dream
of the last curlew flying across the estuary,
of ink stains unfolding slowly through the water.
I wake to inspect the landscape of my hands,
seeing them, as might a seabird or a drone,
so powerless, so small, so far away.

PAT BORAN

THE BROKEN FIELDS

Driving home through the dark
an owl slides past the windscreen.

Fearing I might have hit it
I stop, get out to look –
only an old paper bag.

Only a grieving wind.
Only fields stretching away,
broken fields, aching
in their chemical chains.

MARK ROPER

SEAS SIAR

Lámha san aer   is seas siar
Ón mactíre   a mharaigh tú
Ón madra rua   a lámhach tú

Ón ngráinneog   a leag tú led luas
Ón gcoinín   a nimhnigh tú
Ón ngiorria   a ghabh tú i ngaiste.

Céimnigh siar   ón ngunna,
Ón bhfiailnimh   a leag tú ar an ngort
Ón sreang dhealgach   a chrochais in airde.

Fan fanta siar   go n-athainmhífear tú
Go n-athphlandófar tú
Go dtalamhófar   is go spéireofar tú

Go n-abhannófar   lochófar   is farraigeofar tú
Seas siar go dtí   go n-ionchollófar tú
Líonrith is siansa na mbeach   lá samhraidh.

CEAITÍ NÍ BHEILDIÚIN

STAND BACK

Hands in the air   and stand back
From the wolf   you killed
From the fox   you shot

From the hedgehog   you flattened with speed
From the rabbit   you poisoned
From the hare   you snared

Take a step back   from the gun
From the weedkiller   you spread on the field
From the barbed wire   you erected

Stay stepped back   until you are animal again
Until you are plant again
Until you are earth   and are sky

Until you are river   are lake   are sea
Stand back until   there is incarnate in you
The full and humming tide of bees   in midsummer.

CEAITÍ NÍ BHEILDIÚIN

Translated from the Irish by Paddy Bushe

BLESSINGS

Yesterday, for some reason I couldn't
understand, I suddenly felt starved
of trees and had to make tracks towards
the beeches of Lough Eske to set my heart
at ease and stand there slowly adjusting
myself to the overwhelming presence of all
those trees. It was like coming back among
people again after living for ages
alone and as I reached out and laid my
right hand in blessing on the trunk
of a beech that had the solidity but not
the coldness of stone I knew it for
the living thing it was under the palm
of my hand as surely as I know the living
sensuousness of flesh and bone and my
blessing was returned a hundredfold
before it was time for me to go home.

FRANCIS HARVEY (1925 – 2014)

THE RED DOGS OF WICKLOW

We walked the long road to Templeogue.
Trees line the street,

their rheumatic joints aching dampness and cold.
We found the fox with its dank head

in a puddle, the dark rusty bristles of its fur
hardening into the wind like old nails.

I wanted to lift it over the wall
into a field where grass and leaves

would discolour into its skin as it fell asleep
into the soil, remembering the red dogs of Wicklow

and their snow felt steps into the dark, outside our door.
But we were hesitant, unsure, afraid of disease

and cold with rain. Standing over the fox's body
with no benediction other than the thought

that things are passing from our lives. And so,
we walked on, with our own small hurts

to contend with, until we turned from Terenure
to Templeogue and by some magic I looked

behind to see the fox alive and skulking by a tree,
darting off, it seemed, in every direction possible.

PAUL PERRY

CLOSURE

There is always a door closing, a final out-of-here,
gone-from-your-life moment, the disappearance

of closeness, the togetherness shared
separated, parted, final.

Through a door rapidly diminishing footsteps
bruise our softness, only for it all to lessen

and deaden with each step, until at last
a gulf so wide they are gone, never to be seen again.

And years go by. There is news, a marriage,
a child, a career, a death. Or no news –

they walk away down the plank of a hall
to step off into nothing, to disappear without trace,

continuing that step-by-step away from you,
only to never really leave, so wherever they end up,

or roost in the arms of fate, they continue
to walk the body. Sometimes whispering

in the forgotten reaches of our extremities;
on occasion, stumbling through the briars of dreams

to leave on the tongue in the morning a kiss, or burn,
to shadow slip out of and back into a crowd,

recognized momentarily on a stranger's face,
before they walk on, walk away, keep walking

deeper into the marrow of our bones.

GRACE WELLS

THE THINGS WE KEEP *for Angela O'Kelly*

The things we keep are not the things we need;
the red flag and porcelain horse.
A calendar out of date since John Lennon was shot.
Those heaps that grow in the attic
and the garden shed: schoolbooks
of the old curriculum,
the winner's cup we refuse to relinquish,
a broken statue in salvaged shards;
black vinyl discs – each one with a groove
where the gramophone needle got stuck or skipped.
A carpenter's box with carpenter's tools,
a stack of cards from anniversaries
that added one more year to a love affair,
a marriage, a lost cause.
Soft toys reported missing long ago.
The Kodak camera bought with summer money –
a roll of film locked behind its shutter
holding secrets we'll never know.

The things we keep are not the things we need:
a map of London torn at the crease,
a postcard announcing that *This is the Life*
from someone on leave in the Eternal City.
Armfuls of news gone stale,

junk mail in praise of the local takeaway,
an old diary of pleasurable days,
a catechism with notes in the margins
on the doctrine of grace.
Ticket stubs from opening nights,
a holiday brochure for a land of blue skies
in the south, and keys with no purpose
since a childhood house was left to the dust.

GERARD SMYTH

SKIP

At the end of a long night you drive home
to the house you know is empty, but warm.
You'll let yourself relax, doze by the fire.
Just one stop to make on the way home,
to chuck the rubbish into a factory skip.
You drive quietly into the car park:
the lights are still on in the factory,
you know you're not supposed to use their skip.
Unlock the boot, heave the bag up and away.
Get back in to start the car – find you've no keys.
Realize you've chucked them away with the bag,
into twelve deep feet of tangled rubbish.
You can't ask the factory men for help.
There's no one at home and you're miles from it.
You sit in the car. Misled by a streetlamp
into thinking it's day, a bird starts to sing.
You open the window to hear it better.
It's the robin, you seem to remember,
gets fooled like that. Or is it the chaffinch?

MARK ROPER

THE MOONS

Moons like petals adrift on the stream:
night moon and day moon, moon in eclipse,
slender new moon in the winter sky,
and full harvest moon – a golden ball;
moon of my first breath, my mother's death,
grandfather moon, my father's frail boat,
moon of my lost child, my sister's fall,
moon of my belovèd's waking dream,
moons of my life adrift on the stream.

PAULA MEEHAN

IN IRELAND, I

Every night in Ireland, I
got up in the wee small hours and tidied my luggage,
put on my trousers, a pullover, and stepped out into the dark.
The air that struck my cheeks, the sand and soil under my feet,
all of it was wide-awake. I sensed it in every pore.
The trees were the kind whose juices flow to the tip of
    every twig.
And the birds, every one of them had a soul of its own.
The sea was alive as the first time I saw it,
and the sky as the day it was born.
It was clear, clear beyond a shadow of a doubt
that one day this beautiful world would end.
Just as each and every moment I've felt alive was too rich,
and each and every moment could be the last,
in Ireland, I was always getting ready to move on.

MUTSUO TAKAHASHI
Translated from the Japanese by Mitsuo Ohno & Frank Sewell

IN PRAISE OF POTTERING

Let's not try to seize the moment.
Rather let us rearrange the shed,
put the red flowerpots all in one pile,
the black in another, as we did last year.

Rather than decide we must change diet,
let's drink too much coffee, eat too much cheese.
As for exercise, let us take it as and when
we want, not because we ought.

The improvement of each shining hour?
Let them go by as if inexhaustible.
Marvel how we manage not to trouble them.
There are stars whose light has not reached us yet.

In the Sunflower Nebula each gaseous head
of each cometary knot is twice our solar system's size.
Very little happens for a clear reason.
It is not our fault we grow old and die.

MARK ROPER

PART EIGHT

"I grow old ... I grow old ...
  I shall wear the bottoms of my trousers rolled."
—T.S. Eliot, 'The Love Song of J. Alfred Prufrock'

YOUR NATIVE HOME

You asked me once,
'Where does the wind go?'
I will tell you now.

After it gathers the murmuring sails
Of all the boats in the sea and tugs them to harbour
And lifts every coloured kite in the field,

After it herds the wayward clouds
Back into the sky-pen and spreads the softened pollen
Over the crust of this earth,

After it delivers each longing seed
To its solitary furrow and whistles down
The flute of resting chimneys,

After it mills the wheat in the long-shadowed farmlands
And stretches out to clink the chimes
That hang by a thread on summer porches,

After it swivels the iron-cast weathervanes to caw
Like roosters and sweeps the camphorous leaves
Into the wet ditch,

After it combs the morning fields
And braids the crowns
Of darkening forests,

After it dries yesterday's clothes on your line
And nuzzles around the working nose
Of your sleeping dog,

It finally goes home, where you came from,
And carries your father and mother
To their long-awaited sleep.

GIULIANO NISTRI (b. 1969)

THE DAILY CROSSWORD

The letters are no longer placed inside
the boxes. They were once bang on target:
neat bullet holes all dead straight in a line;
each answer correct and proudly square set.

Her hand was once firm but her words now squirm.
A tremor has become her signature.
The crossword has changed. The spaces that yearn
to be filled now yield to a silent cure.

Somehow we muddle through. I read the clues,
and do my best job of trying to jog
her faltering memory. We both choose
to ignore the fact that she has been robbed

of her keenest skill. Between rounds of pills
and the next day's meal order she replies –
oh, the surprise, when she knows *d'Urberville*,
Analogue or *Shinto*, as if her eyes

still hold the light like a lamp glimpsed through mist.
More often than not, the right words are lost,
her eyes start to drift, and my kindest gift
is to complete the rows down and across

and say, "That's right," as if this can make up
for the countless books bought when I was ill,
the countless answers taught when I got stuck,
and all the other gaps she helped to fill.

ROSS THOMPSON

THE MEADOW

My mother asks me to cut her hair
straight, like the first sward of meadow.
This is the way she wants it, this expert
of directness, this woman from Mayo
who refuses to bend or curve or lose herself
in a grey maze of tangled hair.
I want to layer it, toss it, turn it, choose
to curl this silken skein, this fine coiffure.

And then I see her, a meadow: foxglove,
grasses, burrs and seed-heads, ripened somehow,
ready for fall. Her locks stagger and bend,
my hand starts to cut, caught in a headwind.

ANN JOYCE

MY FATHER PERCEIVED AS A VISION
OF ST. FRANCIS   *for Brendan Kennelly*

It was the piebald horse in next door's garden
frightened me out of a dream
with her dawn whinny. I was back
in the boxroom of the house,
my brother's room now,
full of ties and sweaters and secrets.
Bottles chinked on the doorstep,
the first bus pulled up to the stop.
The rest of the house slept

except for my father. I heard
him rake the ash from the grate,
plug in the kettle, hum a snatch of a tune.
Then he unlocked the back door
and stepped out into the garden.

Autumn was nearly done, the first frost
whitened the slates of the estate.
He was older than I had reckoned,
his hair completely silver,
and for the first time I saw the stoop
of his shoulder, saw that
his leg was stiff. What's he at?
So early and still stars in the west?

They came then: birds
of every size, shape, colour; they came
from the hedges and shrubs,
from eaves and garden sheds,
from the industrial estate, outlying fields,

from Dubber Cross they came
and the ditches of the North Road.

The garden was a pandemonium
when my father threw up his hands
and tossed the crumbs to the air. The sun

cleared O'Reilly's chimney
and he was suddenly radiant,
a perfect vision of St. Francis,
made whole, made young again,
in a Finglas garden.

PAULA MEEHAN

WILSON

Years after all that, we're still out playing,
still together. I'm longer than him now;
now he complains his game is breaking down.
We both know what this means. Ahead, I wait

for him to make up ground between us, and grip
the club the way he showed, my thumb across
the maker's name: *Wilson*. Breathless
when he reaches me, he eyes my hands:

"You're holding on too tight." Is this
his way of saying goodbye or just bustle,
the golfer's artful chatter designed to unsettle?
Either way, it works: up close, where it matters,

he's all lobs and flops and lovely pitches, soft hands
that once saved the lives of stricken children
and still have what they call 'the touch'.
I stab and chop, the ball careening past the target,

first from one side, then the other while he
rolls his one sweetly up to stop. "Getting nearer,"
he consoles. The flag flutters above the cup
but I'm thinking of the other hole, the opened

ground where we'll all finish. His ball
just inches from the drop. Our lives together
a groove worn by my thumb. The *Wil* of Wilson
almost gone; soon all that will be left will be the *son*.

JOHN O'DONNELL

HOLIDAY HOME

The last time my sisters took him
to the holiday home in Leitrim
we had to carry him up and down
the stairs but he was skeletally light.

That Sunday we drove to visit relations,
which we all knew, for him, was the last
time and where an aunt wound up
a reindeer that grotesquely sang

When I'm Sixty-Four. I didn't know
whether to laugh or cry and stepped
outside into the still air and did both.
We drove back the lonely length

of Scarmogue Lough, the pair of us in the back,
an oxygen tank between us as an armrest,
his eyes narrowing on a slope with a ruined cottage
as he wheezed, "someone lived there once".

JOSEPH WOODS

BODY

We never touched, all the years
of our long story, kept our distance.
Your cheekbone – chiseled, bristly –
was a strange land. Even the word *body*
was banned – it never left your mouth.
But now I'm all over you, an octopus
popping pills on your tongue at breakfast,
allowing your false teeth to plop
into my palm at night. I lather soap
on your salt-and-pepper skin, draw
the blade slowly over your jaw, waver
round the small apple. I undress you,
open the shower door, prod you in.
I beg you to send your hand back out,
squeeze shampoo on your palm,
tell you to rub it well into your scalp.
You shiver, cringe, tell me my hands
are icy cold. I never thought I'd see
my father's penis. And after the long haul
of hours spent cajoling you to lie down
under the covers, you grab my hand,
lock it in yours, won't let go.

MARY NOONAN

RED SHOE

Old wards, new wings,
corridors.
One foot in front of the other

brings me to my father.
How small he's grown – a changeling,
a dark thought

in his eyes, under the green.
His old smile
won't wear

but he likes my new red shoes,
notes that one has skinned my heel.
He deplores

the state of play,
the game on TV.
The tall lords come.

Not good, their words, *not
hopeful*. They shake their heads,
cannot foresee release,

not even for a season. Stay.
Swallow the black
seeds of pomegranate.

The afterwards of the car park,
fumbling at the lock,
the sun on my neck.

I put my foot down,
my raw foot, my red
shoe. I would go I would

drive to the end of the earth.

KATHERINE DUFFY

BEDSIDE LOCKER

Starts with Su and ends with Sa,
seven compartments of coloured
pills that dispense each day –
colour-coded for eternity,

resting on the sovereign space
we're often afforded near
the end: the surface
of a bedside locker.

Distinguished by Connemara
marble rosary beads, an eggcup
or Jagermeister shot-glass
of mints and an island of moist

hand-wipes, still life of sorts,
from the miniature silver vessel
of holy-water to the book
with florid endpapers

full of improving quotations
that like most bedside books

was never really for reading.
And the sadness or is it dignity

that attaches to small objects,
not to mention the wardrobe,
whose contents will one day
walk from the charity shop.

JOSEPH WOODS

SEA FRET

The fret came down so thick and fast
you lost all sense of direction.
There was no one there to call to.

You swam round and round
until you thought you would drown.
At last the faintest whisper
of a wave led you back to shore.

You got dressed. Drove home.
Made breakfast. Told no one,
not a single word for twenty years.

You're back inside that fret again,
this time no shore can be found
and you're saying *I'm so sorry,*
I'm so sorry to let you all down.

MARK ROPER

CHERRIES

The ripened cherries roasted where they grew
Each fruit a blood-red world that shrank to brown
When the call came, I went at once to you

The orchards that last month you wandered through
Burst into sweetness as I left for town
The ripened cherries roasted where they grew

I prayed it wasn't, knew it must be true
Packed peaches for you with my mourning gown
When the call came, I went at once to you

This year there'll be no bottling to do
No *eau de vie de cerise* to lay down
The ripened cherries roasted where they grew

It was too late, however fast I flew
To share your last felicity or frown
When the call came, I went at once to you

We harvested the figs, the almonds too,
The golden plums that weighed the branches down
The ripened cherries roasted where they grew
When the call came, I went at once to you

CATHERINE ANN CULLEN

HANDS

Your hands built this house,
bone to brick, a roof and 5 beds
between fields of cows and silage,
hands that brought pipes of water
across the field from the well,
which froze each December
while we shivered in the kitchen
making toast on the heater.
Hands bigger than mine
crooked from engines, black deep in bogs,
the nicotine years and cleaning of pipes,
hands that clattered me,
sent me flying, sent me crying
outside the pub that one time
for robbing cigarettes to smoke in the ditch.
But held me close at football matches
between the frothy roars of towering men.
Hands that hung sheep from a tree
that day when I spied,
behind the shed, the terrored eye

and the blood
and the blood
and the blood
a freezer of mutton to feed us that winter.
Hands that held hers
while the machine pumped her chest,
up and down
up and down
up and down
till they turned it off
and we went home without her.

Hands that wore my shoulders round
the buttonhole I gave you
that day in September when I married him
and told me that you were proud,
hands that are smaller now, quieter now,
that live another life, hands that I see in mine
lines etched, like spiders across milk,
running from time.

CHRIS JONES (b. 1975)

THE HANDS

Today I got my old woman's hands.
I laid my young woman's hands away
in the drawer with my young woman's hair,
that thick dark braid that hung to my waist.
Mind how he swung me once round and round
the garden, to Sergeant Pepper's Band.
That was long ago, a wedding day.
The ring is lost; lost are all my cares.
Old woman's hands now, old woman's face.

PAULA MEEHAN

PUTTING THE CLOCKS FORWARD

The calculation throws me every time,
a simple sum a child could do but, even so,
the brain abandons me,

and suddenly I'm putting up a front.
I'm buying time, reckoning the future in my head
when all the children want to know

is will it mean an hour more or less in bed.
It's nothing, but I feel that jag of terror all the same.
Like when I can't remember who sang what.

Or, unaccountably,
I clean forget a boxer, an actor,
the local beauty's name.

JOHN KELLY

THE OLD PROFESSOR

It's not just that he can't remember
you: he can't recall any of it:
the university, his other
students. I rocked. I reeled. I was knocked
off kilter, as if the child in me
had stepped up to the blackboard and picked
up the chalky duster and wiped her
future lines away, even the bit
where he helps me get sober and clear.

PAULA MEEHAN

SWING *for Prashant Timalsina*

Everybody's feet, they say, should leave the earth
During *Dashain*, and walk the air like the kites
That spool themselves all over the expectant sky.

And so, as goats were brought in droves from hills,
And buses, packed above and beyond all reason,
Swayed their ludicrous way towards villages

All over Nepal, enormous arches of bamboo
Rose and bowed to be tied in graceful support
Of the festival swings in every village.

In Chaudaridara, inadequate with a camera,
I sat in awe-struck envy of the young
Cavorting in sprung rhythm above my head.

You want play swing? you asked at the high
Point of every arc inscribing the waiting sky,
And I drew back with a timid, earthbound

No, I'm too old. Children and the cool teens
Eyeing one another laughed. *But for this week*,
You persisted, *old man also can play swing*.

And the gods know I did – the camera has the proof –
While my legs, amazed at themselves, lifted
And pointed towards the light on distant hills.

I give these words to you as *tikka*, in gratitude
For your seven-year-old wisdom, dear Prashant,
Who taught me how to walk the air again.

PADDY BUSHE

SALT OVER THE SHOULDER

What comes back now are fast walks on Falcarragh's back
    strand,
the sand no longer firm beneath our feet, and plovers
chasing each other in and out of the rolling edge.
Long talks of how we must, one day, leave everything.

Evenings, that winter, we read Akhmatova's poems aloud
and the city of Saint Petersburg filled our sitting room.
And once, when we stepped outside, the stars were the stars
    of Russia
and we remembered a friend who somehow resembled her:

that proud head, at times wrapped in a turban
to show off her long, Modigliani neck. Two lives
lived with the same passion, but one with reckless speed.
Paper. Salt. Stars. When are the sands ever firm?

ANNIE DEPPE (b.1950)

WATCHING HOW IT HAPPENS

Under creased tea-stained tissue-paper skin
the veins on the backs of his hands

surface like the gnarled roots of old trees.
When he rises from a chair or climbs the stairs

he creaks and whistles like the timbers
and rigging of a ship in a storm at sea.

The child that he was is the ghost beginning
to haunt the ruins he thinks is a man.

I watch the old growing old by watching myself.

FRANCIS HARVEY (1925 – 2014)

'WHAT USE YOUR BRIGHT'

What use your bright
    petals now? They fade
in this endless rain
    just … as I have,
gazing out at this life.

ONO NO KOMACHI (Mid 9th century)
Translated from the Japanese by James Hadley and Nell Regan

SATURDAY MORNING

Saturday morning, tea in the pot,
cats on a quilt worn past repair.

Outside the window, the low hills,
stony light, horses in Kearns's field.

Old dried leaf, fresh water. Given cups.
Dust motes in steam. Touch of known skin.

Skin that we're shy of all over again.
That we try to hide from each other.

Which sags, has wrinkles, is mottled.
From which things need to be cut out.

Bodies once so well known to us,
now unknown. Which let us down.

Bodies we're ashamed of, angry about,
find difficult to accept as ours.

Which are no longer possessed
but possess us, at times disgust.

Not the bodies we fell in love with,
couldn't wait to undress.

This was happening all the time
behind the screens of desire.

Bodies grown old and tired, needing
more than ever now to be loved.

Bodies which have grown into each other,
which if separated might not survive.

Tea in the pot. Old dried leaf, fresh water.
Given cups. Us two, in deep.

MARK ROPER

LOVE IN THE GLEN

Never having paraded their love
in the public sense of interlinking hands
and exchanging kisses on the street but
being private in their affections as in
their lives, now that they've grown older and
some of their passion's spent, they compensate
for what they've lost by holding hands in bed.

FRANCIS HARVEY (1925 – 2014)

SEASONS

Though physical desire between them must die
is what even lifelong lovers say, and though their desire –
as if chastened – falls away, I see us kiss
in a room called enfeeblement that is small and bare
and entered by an old, creaky door. There
we undress, ignoring the tarnished eye of the mirror.
There we embrace. Seasons advance – from
winter's crippling cold to where plums cluster, dark
and luscious. From summer's piquant green
to ripe, sun-struck apples. So do sapless sticks flex
and fire themselves afresh to nodding heads
of roses fragranced red and orange and yellow rustling.
The big adventure of the earth rolls out over
one more year. It still can't match our fling. We hold
to our own spring, even in the thin, musty air
behind that narrow door – two sublime slips of a thing.

PATRICK DEELEY

AFTERNOON IN OLHAO

When, after love, the celebratory sun
Slants through the shutters on me

Clinging into your carved back
With my face in your tousled hair,

I nuzzle into the memory of half
A century ago, your uniformed

Back carved into me as I crossbar
You back to school, daring to lean

Into the curve, daring to inhale
Such lifetimes, such fragrances!

PADDY BUSHE

05:40

You're only gone to Dingle, overnight
That's all, but the abrupt gale-driven sleet
On the window hammers that absence home
When you make no shape against the clock's
Lit figures, and I cannot smell your hair.

Awake now, reassured, I click the luxury
Of an undisturbing bedside light to read,
And to lever out the nail that drove
Itself slyly home, that other — at sixty,
It does cross the mind — utter absence.

PADDY BUSHE

149

NEIGHBOURS

Thirty years here – my longest anywhere;
children, small when we moved, one not yet born,
now all grown up and gone.
The garden where they played and washing blew
had trees and hedges to divide
us from our neighbours next door,
an elderly childless pair.
The wife, whom I never knew,
fell ill and died; her widower remained
and lived some years alone.
And then new neighbours came.
Their children fill the air
with noise and cries
just as ours did before;
and now, I realise,
we are to them
the elderly childless pair.
There's only one stage more.
Whichever of us survives
will turn into the one who lives
all on their own next door.

SALLY WHEELER (b. 1937)

ALL THIS

When we grow old, my dear,
and the crows come to get us
(caw-caw, then off with one beat of their wings, into the air),
where will our love be then?

150

Where will this mouth be then that says
something about a broken coffee-machine, rust on the car, a
    visit to the
cardiologist, a filling that has fallen out, the phone bill
or (romantic) about the golden moon
and the rowan-tree in blossom, which explains away all the
    white
lies, the cheatings, and all it doesn't manage to say about the
    child
we never had, and that melts together with your mouth in
    a kiss?

Or these eyes that stare into the green computer screen day
out and day in and that look at you when you take your
    clothes off
as evening draws on:
you put the light out modestly and stand like a silhouette
    with ripe breasts
and thighs against the light that seeps thinly
in through the windows from the cobalt-blue Iceland Sea?
Or these hands that write and write, that put
the snow-shovels in their place and caress you
over your limbs until you burn and want to have me
like a force that smashes into the dams, and I explode
cascading into you, into your womb that was removed by a
    surgeon in Reykjavik?

All this that we call love –
where will it be, when the crows come?
For they will not take us both together. One of us
will be the first to lie out there on the ground dirtied by snow
down by the sea (yellow last year's grass, churned-up spring
    snow)
when the black crows come and pick at the mouth,
the eyes, the hands, the genitals.

That one of us who is left behind the window then, dear,
who wakes in the mornings and does everything
we are familiar with – fetches in *Morgunblaðið* which sits
in the letterbox. Turns on the taps
and looks at himself or herself in the mirror: Does that
    one us then see
something more
than his or her own face there? Will the other face then
shine through the face in the mirror, as abandoned houses
stand and shine by the sea?

KNUT ØDEGÅRD (b. 1945)
Translated from the Norwegian by Brian McNeil

IN MAY THE PARK AND ME REVISITED

The dropouts in the park
Are drinking Bud and Efes
I read the bottle caps
And pull-off tags from cans
Among thin plastic tubes
And tell-tale roaches
              May
Green is all about
And the community of carp
The grey friars of the lake
Are one with children
And their watchers
And all the levels in between
              And I
With those delusive ghosts
Of loneliness and failure

All the empty spaces of the years
Left unredeemed
And all the missing people
Myself among them
                    When
Suddenly being here at all
Amid the sad detritus
Of bottle caps and memories
Beneath my feet
It somehow all seems *yet* –
Too beautiful to leave

MACDARA WOODS (1942 – 2018)

PART NINE

"Do not go gentle into that good night.
Rage, rage against the dying of the light."
—Dylan Thomas, 'Do Not Go Gentle Into That Good Night'

WINTER FUNERAL

The funeral was in Winter,
Without chant or music.

Afterwards, we walked into the frost.
Our footsteps crunched on gravel.

Trees were white and gaunt.
A hapless pheasant crossed our path.

Prayers accomplished, we moved away,
Brushing death from our coats.

PÁDRAIG J. DALY (b. 1943)

PLANS

We made the plans, I made the lists, the phone calls,
the online bookings for the shows, the concerts,
the plans were promising; what was it we had said

we'd do in Spring? – ah yes – Rome, I'd never been,
you didn't care for all the pomp and power
that it flaunted, but agreed you might
give it a chance again, and was there not a small
Greek island? and, yes, definitely Lisbon,
from there an expedition to our children in Brasil.
In April we'd go to Berlin and wander down again
that avenue of flowering cherries where once
the wall had been or stop off at that café
beneath the plane trees where the slow canal
divides in two just past the elegant bridge you loved.
We'd planned to go and listen to the Atos Trio
play Brahms and Schubert in that off-the-beaten-track
rococo venue in Neukölln again around that time –
I'd book the tickets and we'd watch out meanwhile
if the blackbird couple would come back to nest
as usual in the elder tree in our Galway garden
the male waking us punctually with his *saluts matinals*.
And then your birthday celebrations early March
in crocus season, but it was still in winter
during the darkest days and longest nights when
suddenly you took your leave without as much
as asking me my leave on that December day –
that was against our plan, my love, no, never
had that been our plan at all. We'd said we'd walk
along the hunger road over Killary again
when it got warmer and the spring heather bloomed,
also we couldn't miss the Dublin concert
of our grandchild Ruby's post-punk rock band
letting it fly with style and decibel in April, until then
the mornings listening to Bach in bed, and tea, and politics
with our children over dinner – you still wanted to revise
a book you'd worked on before its publication; we'd made
    plans –

you crossed them out – there was so much to do still,
Paris, for instance, the avenues and bridges and
to see the tapestries again in the Musée de Cluny,
the lady and the unicorn amidst the flowers,
also the greyish-green and gold-flecked Grachten
of Amsterdam and your beloved Kreuzberg
with its grotty pubs, you called them punk-baroque,
their studded, pierced, tattooed, stoical
clientele, the balmy summer nights in Görlitzer-
straße below the linden trees with their delirious
narcotic scent, and in the park nearby
a nightingale would strike up loud and clear as if on cue,
that was the plan, also our bi-annual aquarium
trips with grandson Kilian to check on the starfish,
and if the plaice and kite were doing well, cruising
around in their flat otherworldly world,
and if the spider crab – a fierce and crabby-looking thing
would meekly fold its many legs and lie
on Kilian's palm as quiet as a lamb again.
And, as you knew, we hadn't finished the last pages yet
of Saul Friedländer's memoir *Where Memory Leads*,
my beloved, but had planned to finish it quite soon,
yes definitely we had planned to finish it,
yes, without question that had been our plan.

EVA BOURKE

156

PUBLIC

After they had removed your body
and after Ann had tidied the house,
one room was still full of metal and rubber,
all the scaffolding needed to keep you up,
cushions, hoist, frames, wheelchair,
bath-lift, special bed, alarm.
Props waiting for another stage.

It had been such a show. So public.
And you were such a private soul.
You who hated the show of any feeling.
As soon as they began to treat you,
as soon as you were touched, you withdrew.
You'd never have said, but it's there in photos,
the set of the mouth, that puzzle in your eyes.

Like a bird whose broken wing heals
in captivity, but which won't even try
to fly again, you lost the will to live.
All that weakness on show, you grew
more and more helpless. Unbearable,
never to be really on your own.

Unable to find a quiet corner to die,
you hid, in the only place you could,
inside yourself. You left your face behind,
crawled away deeper and deeper.
It took you a long time to manage.
But you got there in the end.

MARK ROPER

COLD

In that white room,
your cold form.

Not stone-cold,
colder than stone,

a cold so intense
it had to be living.

As if, when we lifted
the veil, such cold

could burn colour
back into you, allow

your hands to relax
and receive the sprigs

of rosemary, beech
and winter jasmine

we place on them.

MARK ROPER

MOTHER DIED YESTERDAY

My mother died yesterday
This month of October, five years ago.
It was early in the morning.
She was brought to my sister's house and laid out there.

That night I went to mother's house with
A can of beer and drank it alone.

Then I opened the fridge looking for more beer or anything.
It was full with food.
She could have lived another week without shopping.

I ate some pickles
Some out-of-date yogurt
A spoonful, another spoonful.

Mother died yesterday,
This month of October, five years ago.
That night I laid myself out on her old bed.
My first time home in four years.

ERIKO TSUGAWA-MADDEN (b. 1949)

EVER *for my mother*

And when she was gone
the silver lost its frail brilliance,
the cut glass cobwebbed,
the clocks wound down.

The two brothers
in the story she would read us on Christmas Eve
never made their way in from the blizzard,
never rescued the beggar-woman from the snowdrift
or laid their pennies on the altar,
or found out why the chimes rang.

RICHARD TILLINGHAST

LOST AND FOUND

Sometimes now I see my father
up in Heaven, wandering around
that strange place where he gathers up
what other souls no longer want,
as all his life he gathered
unloved things.

As if on a screen I see
his big frame bend, his bony hands
reach down for a rusted pin,
a nail, a coin from some lost kingdom.
One day it will be the very thing
someone will need.
And when the tears become too much
and this damned bed might be a field,
I sit up wondering how the hell
the world can always find more fools
to lose things and be lost themselves
and carry on.

Then something in my heart gives in,
and I know, as if I'd always known
deep down, that all that trash, that old
Christmas wrapping, those balls of string,
the belts, belt buckles, the left-hand gloves,
the dozens of pairs of worn-out shoes
and toeless socks, the blown light bulbs,
the coils of wire and threadbare screws,
the broken clocks, the plastic bags
folded neatly, the leaking pens
and dried-up markers, the ink-stained rags
and blotting paper, the bashed-in tins

of washers, plasters, needles and lint
were never his at all, were meant
for me.

PAT BORAN

SIN-EATER

He blows on his hands to warm them;
it looks like some ritual, some totem.

Between us, nothing but certainty –
the death-sound in the old woman's throat –

and uncertainty – the priest's whereabouts.
Our whispers summon only a flutter in her eyelids.

Someone mentioned the man down the road
who lives alone, who gives some kind of absolution,

so here we find ourselves with this stout man
in a muddied fleece, who breathes on his hands

and places them on the woman's shoulders.
Tears come first, spilling from her eyes;

those milky shallows that have mirrored us all evening
clear for a moment as he bows his face to hers.

He doesn't look at her tears, allows her gaze to travel
to the ceiling above her bed. Only we invade her privacy.

He says nothing. Not one prayer or word of comfort.
We give him a fifty and wonder.

Some begin to mutter; one man asks what he did.
He tells us that at that late stage she had no voice left,

so he took her sins upon himself,
allowing her to pity him for all he carried.

JESSICA TRAYNOR

THE SHOE BOX COFFIN

My grandad, Joe, laid out his second son
in a card box from Donaghy's Boots and Shoes.
The priest said sacred ground was not for him:
the unbaptized. Joe's face was a dark bruise.
He knew about exclusion, had come south,
well rid of Turnabarson's beggared hill,
his kind long kept from housing and good jobs.
The priest, as he turned away, mentioned God's will.
That night, Joe's friends climbed the high graveyard wall.
Joe slid the box between the gate's grey bars,
threw in their spades and scaled the chilly steel.
They dug in silence under frosted stars
till Joe's hands placed, under the new-made mound,
the shoe box, secret in the sacred ground.

CATHERINE ANN CULLEN

THE INSCRIPTION

'Honour the dust…' wrote Gary Snyder
in my old copy of *No Nature*
before Bella, our beloved dog,
got her teeth into it. Now dog-eared,
oft-thumbed, much annotated, it sits
on a bockety shelf right beside
the well-made box wherein lies her wag,
her bark, her growl, her lick, her rapture
of devotion – her dust we honour.

PAULA MEEHAN

A SINGLE ROSE

I have willed my body to the furthering of science
although I'll not be there
to chronicle my findings
I can imagine all the students
poring over me:
"My God, is that a liver?
And those brown cauliflowers are lungs?"
"Yes, sir, a fine example of how not to live."
"And what about the brain?"
"Alas the brain. I doubt if this poor sample
ever had one." As with his forceps
he extracts a single rose.

LELAND BARDWELL (1922 – 2016)

ANNIVERSARY

I walk down through the glen
to the lake Joe and Eilis have made,
filled by the stream off the hill.

End of October –
in a leaf's slow burn and fall
the sense of a threshold.

I go to drop a late rose
on the water, to watch it steady
on the current and be swept away.

I don't come with a golden bough,
to encounter your shade.
I've no song to bring you back.

I strip and force myself in. The cold
that bites after one or two strokes –
that's what I'm after.

I want to be stopped in my tracks,
speechless, one big shudder.
To have to turn back

because I have to turn back.
I come stooped out of the water.
I remind myself of you.

MARK ROPER

WINTER COAT

Your winter coat hangs inside my wardrobe.
An object memory I cannot trust.
Though it hasn't kept your body warm

in years, been trudged through rain or wrapped
by wind – the kind that animates dead leaves –
it retains your shape, like the cindered frame

of a fire log. Past meaning, it is out
of season, and holds nothing
I can touch, except this strand of hair

woven to the collar, a reminder that marks
only absence, as it glistens still
on this coat that is no longer coat.

LEEANNE QUINN (1978)

MARBHNA OISÍN

i.m. Oisín O'Mahony, naíonán

Mar gur ar éigean ar shroich tú Tir na nÓg
Sular sciobadh arís siar thar farraige thú
Mar nár thuigis riamh draíocht na dúthaí sin
Ná fós arís a bheith dá ceal
Mar ná rabhais riamh faoi gheasa chinn óir
Ná aon chapall bhán faoi smacht na lámha agat
Mar nach raibh agat aon agallamh le seanóirí
Ná seanchas peile, ná camán id lámh agat
Mar gur robáladh an taisce a shamhlaigh d'athair duit

Agus aisling heal do mháthar
Is id dhiaidhse atáthar, Oisín, is tá an saol ar fad
Titithe as a riocht, mar ghaiscíoch ón diallait.

PADDY BUSHE

LAMENT FOR OISÍN

i.m. Oisin O'Mahony, infant

Because you had barely arrived at Tír na nÓg
Before you were swept back out to sea again;
Because you never realised the magic of that place
Nor yet again what it is to lose it;
Because you were never spellbound by golden hair
Nor held the reins of a white horse in your hands;
Because you had never conversed with old men,
Never talked football, nor gripped a hurley;
Because your father was robbed of the treasure he imagined,
And your mother of her brightest dreaming;
We are forlorn, Oisín, and the whole world
Has tumbled to the ground, like a hero from the saddle.

PADDY BUSHE
Translated from the Irish by the author

IN MEMORY OF NAOISE 1993–2002

Sleep, my dearest, sleep and leave us
here to dream of a world we may not
enter with the world in our hearts.

Sleep, my dearest, sleep and in your dreams
know this: the only Heaven we knew
was the Heaven on earth of you.

FRANCIS HARVEY (1925 – 2014)

'NO ROAD BEYOND THE GRAVEYARD'

—Chief Inspector Morse in a novel by Colin Dexter

But the No Road beyond the graveyard
is full of possibilities,
eidetic visions, ghosts,
the valedictory sigh, perhaps.
But when I stand on this No Road,
I am thinking of an old woman
who took the shoes of her son
and polished them, polished them,
till you could see your face in them,
first the left, then the right,
and placed them under the kitchen table
before she died. And the son
stands at the No Road
in the dulled shoes,
in a hopeless frame of mind.
There's no reason for this No Road.
No mention of falling stones,
dangerous cliffs,
likely to flood.
Simply no road,
no five-barred gate,
no 'Dogs Keep Out',
no 'Danger Men at Work',
no 'Closed for Repair',

just, beyond the graveyard,
'No Road'.
No cul de sac, no boreen
no bridle path.
The road doesn't go nowhere,
It simply isn't.
It's quiet too in the graveyard.
No creature, no bird,
no field mouse. Quiet.
Rows upon rows of stones,
crosses, inscriptions, dates,
but quiet. In the end
one keeps one's ghosts
to oneself.

LELAND BARDWELL (1922 – 2016)

ON THE HILL, MY TOMB, MARINE CEMETERY

On the hill, my tomb, marine cemetery
Hidden in the mountain. Ghost-ancestors.
Writing worn off the tombs – second death.
We believe we live in the heart of the living.
They die in their turn. First death.
I am the marine cemetery of another.
The sea rejects the bodies.
I recite the names of the disappeared
My sorrow dries in the sun of forgetting.
Life resumes its course.
Without me.

LANDA WO (b. 1972)

THE OLIVE TREE

There's not a lot we know about the olive tree.
While thousands of rippling leaves shimmer in the sun,
the roots reach down into the dark depths of the earth,
or so we think.
Rows of beard-like roots stretch out to embrace
layers of dead generations from down the centuries,
mixing and merging with their memory, joys and griefs,
or so we think.
The distilled matter seeping out of there
and sucked in by the slender tips of roots
to climb rough paths in the tree-trunk
and flow out lavishly as light,
is a mystery to us.
All we can do is sidle up to the tree
and sit down to rest, read, wait for someone,
talk or, sometimes, make sketches.
One of these days, death will pay us a visit,
and we'll join the serried ranks of the dead.
Siphoned-in by slender roots, we'll be reborn
and flow out of the shimmering leaves as light.
That much we know.

MUTSUO TAKAHASHI

Translated from the Japanese by Mitsuo Ohno & Frank Sewell

ACKNOWLEDGEMENTS & THANKS

The poems in this book are drawn from a variety of Dedalus Press publications, the majority from single-author volumes, details of which may be found on the relevant poet's page on the Dedalus Press website. To save on space, for biographical notes we would direct readers to *www.dedaluspress.com*.

Poems by poets not generally associated with the press are taken from some of our many anthologies, magazines or other multi-author volumes, and include the following publications (in chronological order):
Gennady Alexeyev from *A Night in the Nabokov Hotel: 20 Contemporary Poets from Russia,* ed. Anatoly Kudryavitsky (2006); Celeste Augé, Annie Deppe, Jennifer Matthews, Mary Mullen, Sally Wheeler and Ann Zell from *Landing Place: Immigrant Poets in Ireland,* eds. Eva Bourke and Borbála Faragó (2010); Ulla Hahn from *Coloured Handprints: 20 German-Language Poets,* ed. Anatoly Kudryavitsky (2015); Hanyong Jeong from *The Level Crossing,* ed. Pat Boran (2016); Ruy Bello from *28 Portugese Poets,* ed. Richard Zenith (2015); Lynn Caldwell, Chris Jones, Ben Keatinge, Rafael Mendes, Emma Must, Giuliano Nistri, Eriko Tsugawa-Madden and Christian Wethered from *Writing Home: The 'New Irish' Poets,* eds. Pat Boran and Chiamaka Enyi-Amadi (2019); Sone No Yoshitada, Gyōson, Kisen and Ono No Komachi from *A Gap in the Clouds: A New Translation of the Ogura Hyakunin Isshu,* eds. James Hadley and Nell Regan (2021.

Finally, we wish to thank all the poets and copyright holders who gave permission to republish their work in this volume.

DEDALUS PRESS

Named for James Joyce's literary alter ego,
Dedalus Press is one of Ireland's longest running
and best-known literary imprints, dedicated to
contemporary Irish poetry, and to poetry
from around the world in English translation.

For more information, or to purchase copies
of this or other Dedalus Press titles,
please visit us at *www.dedaluspress.com*.

*"One of the most outward-looking
poetry presses in Ireland and the UK"*
—UNESCO.org

Poetry Matters:
Spread the Word

9 781915 629067